SAS® Macro Language 1: Essentials

Course Notes

SAS® Macro Language 1: Essentials Course Notes was developed by Jim Simon and Theresa Stemler. Additional contributions were made by Susan Farmer, Cynthia Johnson, Lynn Mackay, Bill Powers, Warren Repole, Roger Speas, Roger Staum, and Kenny Sucher. Editing and production support was provided by the Curriculum Development and Support Department.

SAS® Macro Language 1: Essentials Course Notes

Book code E1501, course code LWMAC1/MAC1, prepared date 15Jun2009.   LWMAC1_002

ISBN 978-1-60764-252-7

Table of Contents

Course Description vii

Prerequisites viii

Chapter 1   Introduction **1-1**

1.1   Course Logistics 1-3

1.2   Purpose of the Macro Facility 1-7

1.3   Program Flow 1-13

        Exercises 1-27

1.4   Chapter Review 1-29

1.5   Solutions 1-30

        Solutions to Exercises 1-30

        Solutions to Student Activities (Polls/Quizzes) 1-31

        Solutions to Chapter Review 1-32

Chapter 2   Macro Variables **2-1**

2.1   Introduction to Macro Variables 2-3

2.2   Automatic Macro Variables 2-6

2.3   Macro Variable References 2-10

        Exercises 2-28

2.4   User-Defined Macro Variables 2-30

        Exercises 2-46

2.5   Delimiting Macro Variable References 2-48

        Exercises 2-56

2.6   Macro Functions 2-58

        Exercises 2-74

2.7   Chapter Review..2-76

2.8   Solutions 2-77

　　　　Solutions to Exercises 2-77

　　　　Solutions to Student Activities (Polls/Quizzes)...2-84

　　　　Solutions to Chapter Review 2-90

Chapter 3   Macro Definitions **3-1**

3.1   Defining and Calling a Macro...3-3

　　　　Exercises...3-19

3.2   Macro Parameters 3-21

　　　　Exercises...3-36

3.3   Macro Storage (Self-Study) 3-39

　　　　Exercises...3-50

3.4   Chapter Review..3-52

3.5   Solutions 3-53

　　　　Solutions to Exercises 3-53

　　　　Solutions to Student Activities (Polls/Quizzes) 3-62

　　　　Solutions to Chapter Review 3-64

Chapter 4   DATA Step and SQL Interfaces..**4-1**

4.1   Creating Macro Variables in the DATA Step 4-3

　　　　Exercises...4-23

4.2   Indirect References to Macro Variables 4-26

　　　　Demonstration: Indirect References to Macro Variables (Self-Study)....................4-39

　　　　Exercises...4-40

4.3   Retrieving Macro Variables in the DATA Step (Self-Study)...........................4-43

　　　　Exercises...4-47

4.4   Creating Macro Variables in SQL..4-49

Exercises..4-58

4.5   Chapter Review..4-62

4.6   Solutions 4-63

        Solutions to Exercises 4-63

        Solutions to Student Activities (Polls/Quizzes)......................................4-72

        Solutions to Chapter Review..4-75

Chapter 5   Macro Programs 5-1

5.1   Conditional Processing 5-3

        Exercises..5-18

5.2   Parameter Validation 5-20

        Exercises..5-27

5.3   Iterative Processing...5-30

        Exercises..5-45

5.4   Global and Local Symbol Tables..5-48

        Exercises..5-66

5.5   Chapter Review..5-70

5.6   Solutions 5-71

        Solutions to Exercises 5-71

        Solutions to Student Activities (Polls/Quizzes)......................................5-84

        Solutions to Chapter Review..5-88

Chapter 6   Learning More.. 6-1

6.1   SAS Resources...6-3

6.2   Beyond This Course..6-6

Appendix A   Supplemental Materials A-1

A.1   Program Flow A-3

Appendix B   Index **B-1**

Course Description

This course focuses on the components of the SAS macro facility and how to design, write, and debug macro systems. Emphasis is placed on understanding how programs with macro code are processed.

To learn more...

For information on other courses in the curriculum, contact the SAS Education Division at 1-800-333-7660, or send e-mail to training@sas.com. You can also find this information on the Web at support.sas.com/training/ as well as in the Training Course Catalog.

For a list of other SAS books that relate to the topics covered in this Course Notes, USA customers can contact our SAS Publishing Department at 1-800-727-3228 or send e-mail to sasbook@sas.com. Customers outside the USA, please contact your local SAS office.

Also, see the Publications Catalog on the Web at support.sas.com/pubs for a complete list of books and a convenient order form.

Prerequisites

Before attending this course, you should have completed the SAS® Programming 2: Data Manipulation Techniques course or have equivalent knowledge. Specifically, you should be able to

- use a DATA step to read from or write to a SAS data set or external file
- use DATA step programming statements such as IF-THEN/ELSE, DO WHILE, DO UNTIL, and iterative DO
- use SAS data set options such as DROP=, KEEP=, and OBS=
- use character functions such as SUBSTR, SCAN, INDEX, and UPCASE
- form subsets of data using the WHERE clause
- create and use SAS date values and constants
- use SAS procedures such as SORT, PRINT, CONTENTS, MEANS, FREQ, TABULATE, and CHART.

Chapter 1   Introduction

1.1   Course Logistics **1-3**

1.2   Purpose of the Macro Facility **1-7**

1.3   Program Flow **1-13**

       Exercises 1-27

1.4   Chapter Review **1-29**

1.5   Solutions **1-30**

       Solutions to Exercises 1-30

       Solutions to Student Activities (Polls/Quizzes) 1-31

       Solutions to Chapter Review 1-32

1.1 Course Logistics

Objectives

- Explain the naming convention that is used for the course files.
- Compare the three levels of exercises that are used in the course.
- Describe at a high level how data is used and stored at Orion Star Sports & Outdoors.
- Navigate to the Help facility.

3

Filename Conventions

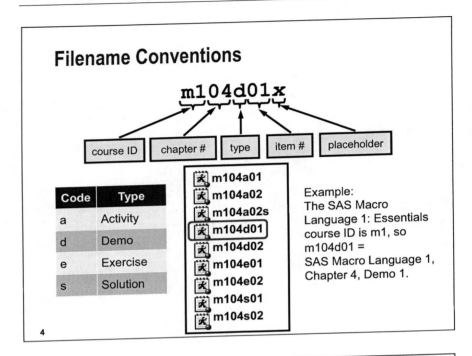

Code	Type
a	Activity
d	Demo
e	Exercise
s	Solution

Example:
The SAS Macro
Language 1: Essentials
course ID is m1, so
m104d01 =
SAS Macro Language 1,
Chapter 4, Demo 1.

4

Three Levels of Exercises

Level 1	The exercise mimics an example presented in the section.
Level 2	Less information and guidance are provided in the exercise instructions.
Level 3	Only the task you are to perform or the results to be obtained are provided. Typically, you will need to use the Help facility.

✐ You are not expected to complete all of the exercises
in the time allotted. Choose the exercise or exercises
that are at the level you are most comfortable with.

5

Orion Star Sports & Outdoors

Orion Star Sports & Outdoors is a fictitious global sports and outdoors retailer with traditional stores, an online store, and a large catalog business.

The corporate headquarters is located in the United States with offices and stores in many countries throughout the world.

Orion Star has about 1,000 employees and 90,000 customers, processes approximately 150,000 orders annually, and purchases products from 64 suppliers.

6

Orion Star Data

As is the case with most organizations, Orion Star has a large amount of data about its customers, suppliers, products, and employees. Much of this information is stored in transactional systems in various formats.

Using applications and processes such as SAS Data Integration Studio, this transactional information was extracted, transformed, and loaded into a data warehouse.

Data marts were created to meet the needs of specific departments such as Marketing.

7

Macro Language Help Facility

Launch a SAS session and navigate to the Help facility
for the macro language.

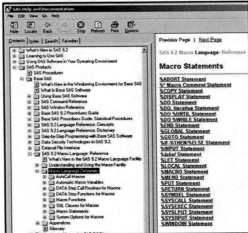

8

SAS online documentation:

http://support.sas.com/documentation/onlinedoc/base/index.html

1.01 Poll

Were you able to access the Help facility?

O Yes
O No

10

1.2 Purpose of the Macro Facility

Objectives

- State the purpose of the macro facility.
- View examples of macro applications.

13

Purpose of the Macro Facility

The *macro facility* is a text processing facility for automating and customizing SAS code. The macro facility helps minimize the amount of SAS code you must type to perform common tasks.

The macro facility supports the following:
- symbolic substitution within SAS code
- automated production of SAS code
- dynamic generation of SAS code
- conditional construction of SAS code

14

Purpose of the Macro Facility

The macro facility enables you to do the following:
- create and resolve **macro variables** anywhere within a SAS program
- write and call **macro programs** (**macro definitions** or **macros**) that generate custom SAS code

15

Substituting System Values

Example: Include system values within SAS footnotes.

```
proc print data=orion.customer;
title "Customer List";
footnote1 "Created 10:24 Monday, 31MAR2008";
footnote2 "on the WIN System Using SAS 9.2";
run;
```

Automatic macro variables store system values that can be used to avoid hardcoding.

16

Substituting User-Defined Values

Example: Reference the same value repeatedly
throughout a program.

```
proc freq data=orion.order_fact;
   where year(order_date)=2008;
   table order_type;
   title "Order Types for 2008";
run;
proc means data=orion.order_fact;
   where year(order_date)=2008;
   class order_type;
   var Total_Retail_Price;
   title "Price Statistics for 2008";
run;
```

User-defined macro variables enable you to define a value once and substitute that value repeatedly within a program.

17

Conditional Processing

Example: Generate a detailed report on a daily basis.
Generate an additional report every Friday,
summarizing data on a weekly basis.

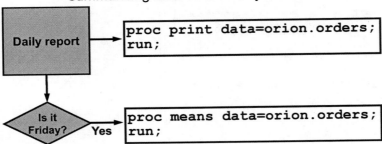

```
proc print data=orion.orders;
run;
```

```
proc means data=orion.orders;
run;
```

A *macro program* can **conditionally** execute selected
portions of a SAS program based on user-defined
conditions.

18

Repetitive Processing

Example: Generate a similar report each year from
2008 to 2010.

```
proc print data=orion.year2008;
run;
```

```
proc print data=orion.year2009;
run;
```

```
proc print data=orion.year2010;
run;
```

A macro program can **generate SAS code repetitively**,
substituting different values with each iteration.

19

Data-Driven Applications

Example: Create separate subsets of a selected data set
for each unique value of a selected variable.

```
data AU CA DE IL TR US ZA;
   set orion.customer;
   select(country);
      when("AU")  output AU;
      when("CA")  output CA;
      when("DE")  output DE;
      when("IL")  output IL;
      when("TR")  output TR;
      when("US")  output US;
      when("ZA")  output ZA;
      otherwise;
   end;
run;
```

A macro program can **generate data-driven code**.

20

Efficiency of Macro-Based Applications

The macro facility can reduce both the **development time**
and the **maintenance time** for programs.

SAS code generated by macro techniques

- does not compile or execute faster than any other
  SAS code
- depends on the efficiency of the underlying SAS code,
  regardless of how the SAS code was generated.

21

Developing Macro Applications

If a macro application generates SAS code, use a five-step approach.

1. Write and debug the SAS program without macro coding.
2. Generalize the program by replacing hardcoded values with macro variable references. `Chapter 2`
3. Create a macro definition with macro parameters. `Chapter 3`
4. Add macro-level programming for conditional and iterative processing. `Chapter 5`
5. Add data-driven customization. `Chapter 5`

The five-step approach enables rapid development and debugging, because syntax and logic at the SAS code level is isolated from syntax and logic at the macro level.

22

1.02 Quiz

The macro facility is a __text__ processing facility for automating and customizing SAS code.

24

1.3 Program Flow

Objectives

- Identify the tokens in a SAS program.
- Describe how a SAS program is tokenized, compiled, and executed.

28

Program Flow

A SAS program can be any combination of the following:

- DATA steps and PROC steps
- global statements
- SAS Component Language (SCL)
- Structured Query Language (SQL)
- SAS macro language

When you submit a program, it is copied to a memory location called the *input stack*.

29

Program Flow

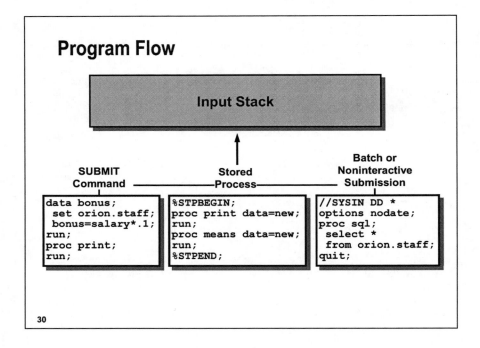

```
data bonus;
 set orion.staff;
 bonus=salary*.1;
run;
proc print;
run;
```

```
%STPBEGIN;
proc print data=new;
run;
proc means data=new;
run;
%STPEND;
```

```
//SYSIN DD *
options nodate;
proc sql;
 select *
 from orion.staff;
quit;
```

30

Program Flow

When SAS code is in the input stack, a component of SAS called the *word scanner* does the following:

- reads the text in the input stack, character by character, left to right, top to bottom
- breaks the text into fundamental units called *tokens*

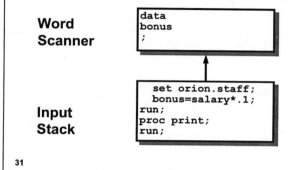

Word Scanner

```
data
bonus
;
```

Input Stack

```
  set orion.staff;
  bonus=salary*.1;
run;
proc print;
run;
```

31

Program Flow

The word scanner passes the tokens, one at a time, to the appropriate *compiler*, as the compiler demands.

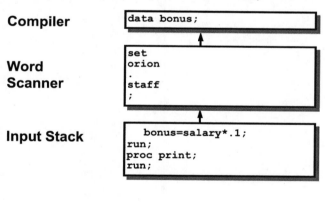

Compiler

```
data bonus;
```

Word Scanner

```
set
orion
.
staff
;
```

Input Stack

```
    bonus=salary*.1;
run;
proc print;
run;
```

32

Program Flow

The compiler does this:
- requests tokens until it receives a semicolon
- performs a syntax check on the statement
- repeats this process for each statement

SAS does this:
- suspends compilation when a step boundary is encountered
- executes the compiled code if there are no compilation errors
- repeats this process for each step

33

Tokenization

The word scanner recognizes four classes of tokens:
- name tokens
- special tokens
- literal tokens
- number tokens

34

Name Tokens

Name tokens contain one or more characters beginning with a letter or underscore and continuing with underscores, letters, or numerals.

Examples: infile

_n_

item3

univariate

dollar10.2

✎ Format and informat names contain a period.

35

Special Tokens

Special tokens can be any character, or combination of characters, other than a letter, numeral, or underscore.

Examples: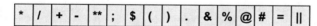

| * | / | + | - | ** | ; | $ | (|) | . | & | % | @ | # | = | ‖ |

This list is not all-inclusive.

36

Literal Tokens

A *literal token* is a string of characters enclosed in single or double quotation marks.

Examples: 'Any text'
             "Any text"

✐   The string is treated as a unit by the compiler.

37

Number Tokens

Number tokens can be
- integer numbers, including SAS date constants
- floating point numbers, containing a decimal point and/or exponent.

Examples: 3
             3.
             3.5
             -3.5
             '01jan2009'd
             5E8
             7.2E-4

38

Tokenization

A token ends when the word scanner detects one of the following:

- the beginning of another token
- a blank after a token

Blanks are **not** tokens. Blanks **delimit** tokens.

The maximum length of a token is 32,767 characters.

39

Example

Input Stack   `var x1-x10                 z         ;`

Tokens
1. var
2. x1
3. -
4. x10
5. z
6. ;

40

Example

Input Stack   `title 'Report for May';`

Tokens
1. title
2. 'Report for May'
3. ;

41

1.03 Multiple Choice Poll

When is SAS code executed?

a. Before the input stack
b. After the input stack and before the word scanner
c. After the word scanner and before compilation
d. At a step boundary after compilation
e. None of the above

43

Macro Triggers

During word scanning, two token sequences are recognized as *macro triggers*:

- *%name-token*   a macro statement, function, or call
- *&name-token*   a macro variable reference

The word scanner passes macro triggers to the *macro processor*.

45

Program Flow (Review)

Recall the program flow presented earlier.

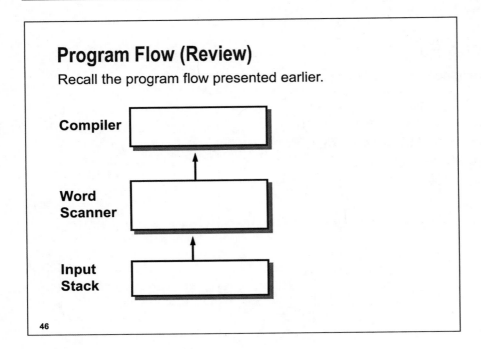

46

The Macro Processor

The macro processor executes macro triggers, including macro language statements, macro functions, macro calls, and macro variable resolution, requesting tokens as necessary.

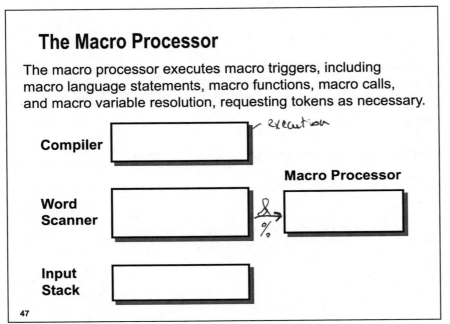

47

Macro Statements

The following are characteristics of *macro statements*:
- begin with a percent sign (%) followed by a name token
- end with a semicolon
- represent macro triggers
- are executed by the macro processor

48

The %PUT Statement

The %PUT statement does the following:

- writes text to the SAS log
- writes to column one of the next line
- writes a blank line if no text is specified

General form of the %PUT statement:

%PUT *text*;

Quotation marks are not required around text in %PUT statements. %PUT statements are valid in open code (anywhere in a SAS program).

49

The %PUT Statement

Example: Use a %PUT statement to write text to the SAS log.

Partial SAS Log

```
12 %put Hi Mom!;
Hi Mom!
```

50

Program Flow

The %PUT statement is submitted.

Compiler

Macro Processor

Word Scanner

Input Stack `%put Hi Mom!;`

51

...

Program Flow

The statement is tokenized.

Compiler

Macro Processor

Word Scanner
```
%
put
Hi
Mom
!
;
```

Input Stack

52

...

Program Flow

When a macro trigger is encountered, it is passed to the macro processor for evaluation.

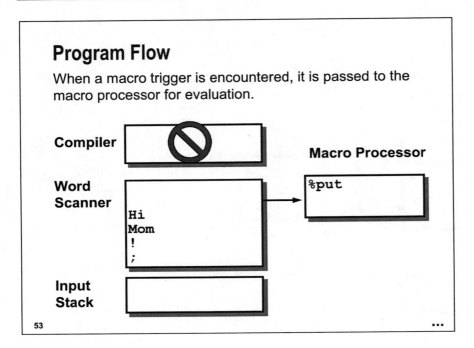

Macro Processor

Compiler

Word Scanner

```
Hi
Mom
!
;
```

```
%put
```

Input Stack

53   ...

Program Flow

The macro processor requests tokens until a semicolon is encountered. It then executes the macro statement.

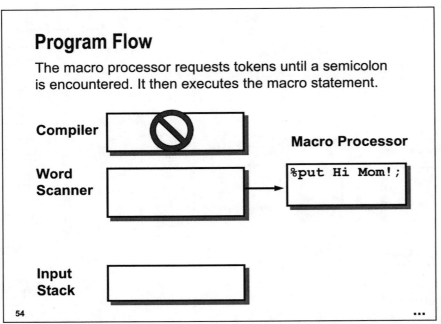

Macro Processor

Compiler

Word Scanner

```
%put Hi Mom!;
```

Input Stack

54   ...

 **Exercises**

Level 1

1. **Writing Text to the SAS Log with the %PUT Statement**

   Submit a %PUT statement that writes your name to the SAS log.

2. **Writing NOTE, WARNING, and ERROR Messages to the SAS Log with the %PUT Statement**

   a. Open the program **m101e02** shown below into the Editor window.

   ```
   %put NOTE: Is this a SAS note?;
   %put WARNING: Is this a SAS warning?;
   %put ERROR: Is this a SAS error?;
   ```

   b. Submit the program and review the results in the SAS log. What is unusual about the results?

   _____

   _____

   _____

   c. Replace the colon so that a hyphen follows the keywords NOTE, WARNING, and ERROR. Submit the program and review the results in the SAS log. How did that change the results?

   _____

   _____

   _____

   d. Modify the program so that the keywords NOTE, WARNING, and ERROR are in lowercase. Submit the program and review the results in the SAS log. Did the change affect the results?

   _____

   _____

   _____

Level 2

3. Writing Special Characters to the SAS Log with the %PUT Statement

   a. Submit the following %PUT statement:

```
%put Can you display a semicolon ; in your %PUT statement?;
```

   b. Does the %PUT statement generate any text? If so, what is the text displayed in the SAS log?

_____

_____

   c. Does the %PUT statement generate any error messages? If so, what is the cause of the error?

_____

_____

   d. Is the second %PUT interpreted as text or a macro keyword?

_____

_____

1.4   Chapter Review

Chapter Review

1. What are the stages of program flow for a SAS program with no macro triggers?

    Input Stack, Word Scanner, Compiler

2. What are the four token categories?

    name, special, literal, number

3. What are the two macro triggers?

    % name - token (macro statement)
    & name - token (macro variable)

57

1.5 Solutions

Solutions to Exercises

1. **Writing Text to the SAS Log with the %PUT Statement**

    ```
    %put Jane Doe;
    ```

2. **Writing NOTE, WARNING, and ERROR Messages to the SAS Log with the %PUT Statement**

    a. Open the program into the Editor window.

    ```
    %put NOTE: Is this a SAS note?;
    %put WARNING: Is this a SAS warning?;
    %put ERROR: Is this a SAS error?;
    ```

    b. The keywords NOTE, WARNING, and ERROR make the results of the %PUT statements resemble standard SAS NOTE, WARNING, and ERROR messages. Depending on the operating environments, the messages might be color-coded or just displayed in bold.

    c. The hyphen forces the keywords NOTE, WARNING, and ERROR to be suppressed.

    d. The keywords NOTE, WARNING, and ERROR are case-sensitive and do not have the desired effect when typed in lowercase.

3. **Writing Special Characters to the SAS Log with the %PUT Statement**

    a. Submit the following %PUT statement:

    ```
    %put Can you display a semicolon ; in your %PUT statement?;
    ```

    b. The first semicolon in the %PUT statement is treated as special token, not as plain text, and ends the statement. The %PUT statement generates the following text:

    Partial SAS Log

    ```
    1       %put Can you display a semicolon ; in your %PUT statement?;
    Can you display a semicolon
    ```

    c. An error message is generated after the first semicolon because the word IN is interpreted as an invalid keyword.

    Partial SAS Log

    ```
    1     %put Can you display a semicolon ; in your %PUT statement?;
                                              --
                                              180
    ERROR 180-322: Statement is not valid or it is used out of proper order.
    ```

    d. Because of the first semicolon, the second %PUT is interpreted as a macro keyword that generates the following text:

    Partial SAS Log

    ```
    statement?
    ```

    > The method for interpreting special tokens as plain text is addressed later in the course.

Solutions to Student Activities (Polls/Quizzes)

1.02 Quiz – Correct Answer

The macro facility is a __text__ processing facility for automating and customizing SAS code.

25

1.03 Multiple Choice Poll – Correct Answer

When is SAS code executed?

a. Before the input stack
b. After the input stack and before the word scanner
c. After the word scanner and before compilation
d. At a step boundary after compilation
e. None of the above

44

Solutions to Chapter Review

Chapter Review - Correct Answers

1. What are the stages of program flow for a SAS program with no macro triggers?

   Input Stack > Word Scanner > Compiler

2. What are the four token categories?

   Name tokens, number tokens, special tokens, literal tokens

3. What are the two macro triggers?

   &*name-token*, %*name-token*

58

Chapter 2 Macro Variables

2.1 **Introduction to Macro Variables**...**2-3**

2.2 **Automatic Macro Variables**..**2-6**

2.3 **Macro Variable References**..**2-10**

      Exercises...2-28

2.4 **User-Defined Macro Variables**..**2-30**

      Exercises...2-46

2.5 **Delimiting Macro Variable References** **2-48**

      Exercises...2-56

2.6 **Macro Functions**..**2-58**

      Exercises...2-74

2.7 **Chapter Review**..**2-76**

2.8 **Solutions** **2-77**

      Solutions to Exercises 2-77

      Solutions to Student Activities (Polls/Quizzes) 2-84

      Solutions to Chapter Review 2-90

2.1 Introduction to Macro Variables

Objectives

- Describe what macro variables store and where macro variables are stored.
- Identify the two types of macro variables.

3

Macro Variables

Macro variables store text, including the following:

- complete or partial SAS steps
- complete or partial SAS statements

Macro variables are called *symbolic variables* because SAS programs can reference macro variables as symbols for SAS code.

4

Global Symbol Table

Macro variables are stored in a memory area called the *global symbol table.* When SAS is invoked, the global symbol table is created and initialized with **automatic macro variables**.

	Global Symbol Table
Automatic Variables	SYSDATE 09NOV07 SYSDATE9 09NOV2007 SYSDAY Friday SYSTIME 10:47 SYSUSERID joeuser . . . .

5

Global Symbol Table

User-defined macro variables can be added to the global symbol table.

	Global Symbol Table
	. . . .
Automatic Variables	SYSTIME 10:47 SYSUSERID joeuser . .
User-Defined Variables	OFFICE Sydney DATE1 25may2008 UNITS 4

6

Macro Variables

Macro variables in the global symbol table

- are global in scope (always available)
- have a minimum length of 0 characters (*null value*)
- have a maximum length of 65,534 (64K) characters
- store numeric tokens as text.

7

2.01 Quiz

What are the two kinds of macro variables?

Where are macro variables stored?

9

2.2 Automatic Macro Variables

Objectives

- Identify selected automatic macro variables.
- Display automatic macro variables in the SAS log.

13

Automatic Macro Variables

The following are true for automatic macro variables:

- system-defined
- created at SAS invocation
- global in scope (always available)
- assigned values by SAS
- can be assigned values by the user in some cases

14

System-Defined Automatic Macro Variables

Some automatic macro variables have fixed values that are set at SAS invocation:

Name	Description
SYSDATE	Date of SAS invocation (17JAN08).
SYSDATE9	Date of SAS invocation (17JAN2008).
SYSDAY	Day of the week of SAS invocation (Friday).
SYSTIME	Time of SAS invocation (13:39).
SYSSCP	Operating system abbreviation (WIN, OS, HP 64, etc.).
SYSVER	Release of SAS software (9.2).
SYSUSERID	Login or user ID of current SAS process.

15

System-Defined Automatic Macro Variables

Some automatic macro variables have values that change automatically based on submitted SAS statements:

Name	Description
SYSLAST	Name of the most recently created SAS data set in the form *libref.name*. If no data set has been created, the value is _NULL_.
SYSPARM	Value specified at SAS invocation.
SYSERR	SAS DATA or PROC step return code (0=success).
SYSLIBRC	LIBNAME statement return code (0=success).

16

Automatic Macro Variables

Example: Write the names and values of all automatic
macro variables to the SAS log using the
AUTOMATIC argument of the %PUT
statement.

```
%put _automatic_ ;
```

17

Automatic Macro Variables

Partial SAS Log

```
12    %put _automatic_;
AUTOMATIC AFDSID 0
AUTOMATIC AFDSNAME
AUTOMATIC AFLIB
AUTOMATIC AFSTR1
AUTOMATIC AFSTR2
AUTOMATIC FSPBDV
AUTOMATIC SYSBUFFR
AUTOMATIC SYSCC 3000
AUTOMATIC SYSCHARWIDTH 1
AUTOMATIC SYSCMD
AUTOMATIC SYSDATE 05FEB08
AUTOMATIC SYSDATE9 05FEB2008
```

The macro variables SYSDATE, SYSDATE9, and
SYSTIME store character strings, **not** SAS date or
time values.

18

2.02 Quiz

Submit the following statement:

```
%put _automatic_;
```

What is the value of **SYSSCPL**?

20

2.3 Macro Variable References

Objectives

- Explain how macro variable references are handled by the word scanner and macro processor.

24

Macro Variable References

The following are true for macro variable references:

- begin with an ampersand (&) followed by a macro variable name
- can appear anywhere in your program
- are not case sensitive
- are also called symbolic references
- represent macro triggers
- are passed to the macro processor

When the macro processor receives a macro variable reference, it does the following:

- searches the symbol table for the macro variable
- resolves the macro variable by substituting its value
- issues a warning to the SAS log if the macro variable is not found in the symbol table

25

Macro Variable References

Example: Write the day of the week to the SAS log.

Partial SAS Log

```
12    %put Today is &sysday;
Today is Tuesday
```

26

Substitution within a Macro Statement

Compiler

Macro Processor

Word Scanner

Input Stack

```
%put Today is &sysday;
```
Trigger   Trigger

Symbol Table	
SYSDAY	Tuesday
SYSLAST	_NULL_

27

...

Substitution within a Macro Statement

When a macro trigger is encountered, it is passed to the macro processor for evaluation.

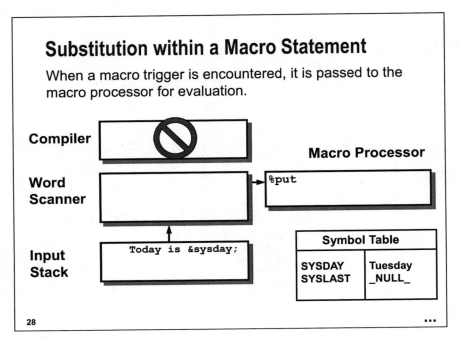

Substitution within a Macro Statement

The macro processor requests tokens until a semicolon is encountered.

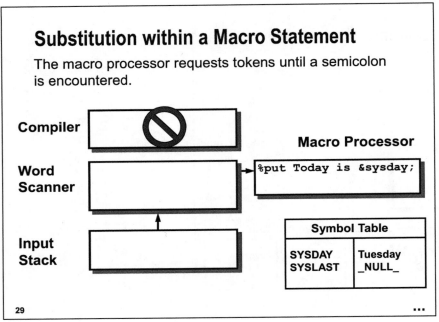

Substitution within a Macro Statement

The macro variable reference triggers the macro processor to search the symbol table for the reference.

Compiler

Word Scanner

Macro Processor

`%put Today is &sysday;`

Input Stack

Symbol Table	
SYSDAY SYSLAST	Tuesday _NULL_

30   ...

Substitution within a Macro Statement

The macro processor resolves the macro variable reference, substituting its value.

Compiler

Word Scanner

Macro Processor

`%put Today is Tuesday;`

Input Stack

Symbol Table	
SYSDAY SYSLAST	Tuesday _NULL_

31   ...

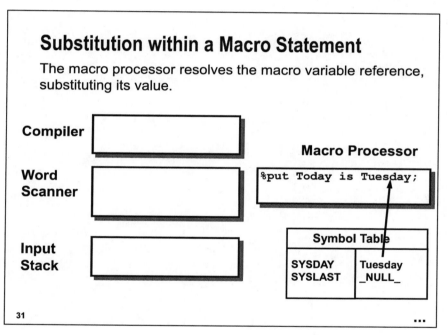

Substitution within a Macro Statement

The macro processor executes the %PUT statement,
writing the resolved text to the SAS log.

Compiler

**Word
Scanner**

**Input
Stack**

Macro Processor

```
%put Today is Tuesday;
```

Symbol Table	
SYSDAY	Tuesday
SYSLAST	_NULL_

32

2.03 Quiz

Submit program **m102d01a**.

What are the footnotes in the PROC FREQ output?

```
proc freq data=orion.Customer;
   table Country / nocum;
   footnote1 'Created &systime &sysday, &sysdate9';
   footnote2 'By user &sysuserid on system &sysscpl';
run;
```

34

Substitution within a SAS Literal

SAS Output

```
         Customer Country

Country    Frequency      Percent

AU             8          10.39
CA            15          19.48
DE            10          12.99
IL             5           6.49
TR             7           9.09
US            28          36.36
ZA             4           5.19

Created &systime &sysday, &sysdate9
By user &sysuserid on system &sysscpl
```

The word scanner does not tokenize literals enclosed in single quotation marks, so macro variables do not resolve.

36

Substitution within a SAS Literal

Example: Substitute system information in footnotes.

```
proc freq data=orion.Customer;
    table Country / nocum;
    footnote1 "Created &systime &sysday, &sysdate9";
    footnote2 "By user &sysuserid on system &sysscp1";
run;
```

To reference macro variables within a literal, enclose the
literal in double quotation marks.

m102d01b

37

Substitution within a SAS Literal

PROC FREQ Output

```
              Customer Country

Country     Frequency        Percent

AU                  8          10.39
CA                 15          19.48
DE                 10          12.99
IL                  5           6.49
TR                  7           9.09
US                 28          36.36
ZA                  4           5.19


Created 10:47 Friday, 09NOV2007
By user joeuser on system XP_PRO
```

38

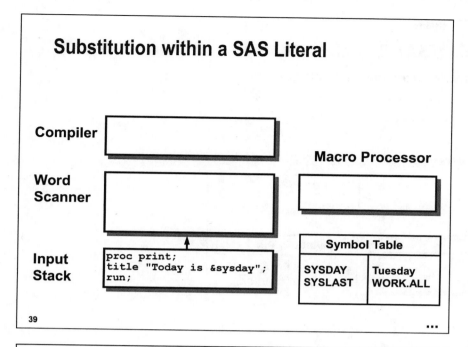

Substitution within a SAS Literal

Compiler	
	Macro Processor

Word Scanner	

| **Input Stack** | `proc print;`
`title "Today is &sysday";`
`run;` |

Symbol Table	
SYSDAY	Tuesday
SYSLAST	WORK.ALL

39

...

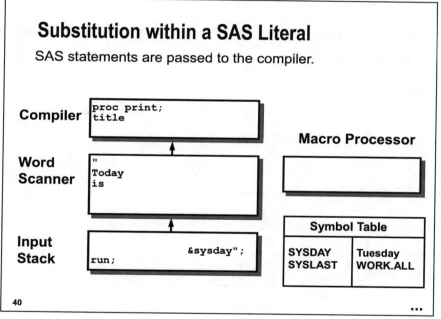

Substitution within a SAS Literal

SAS statements are passed to the compiler.

Compiler	`proc print;` `title`
	Macro Processor

Word Scanner	`"`
	`Today`
	`is`

| **Input Stack** | `run;`   `&sysday";` |

Symbol Table	
SYSDAY	Tuesday
SYSLAST	WORK.ALL

40

...

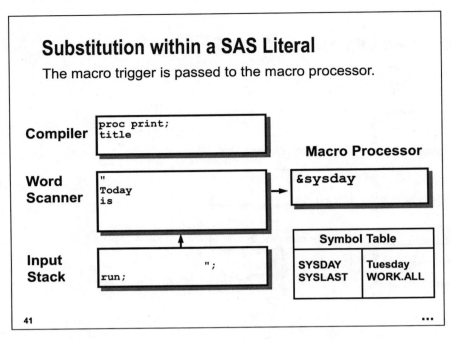

Substitution within a SAS Literal

The macro trigger is passed to the macro processor.

Compiler
```
proc print;
title
```

Macro Processor

Word Scanner
```
"
Today
is
```

```
&sysday
```

Input Stack
```
                    ";
run;
```

Symbol Table

| SYSDAY | Tuesday |
| SYSLAST | WORK.ALL |

41   ...

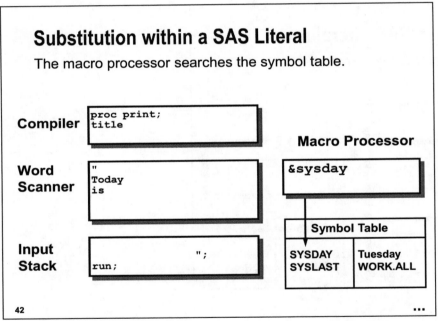

Substitution within a SAS Literal

The macro processor searches the symbol table.

Compiler
```
proc print;
title
```

Macro Processor

Word Scanner
```
"
Today
is
```

```
&sysday
```

Input Stack
```
                    ";
run;
```

Symbol Table

| SYSDAY | Tuesday |
| SYSLAST | WORK.ALL |

42   ...

Substitution within a SAS Literal

The resolved reference is passed back to the input stack.

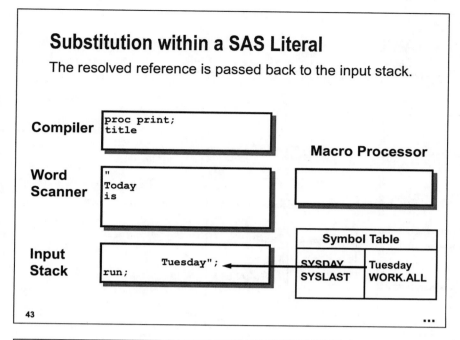

Substitution within a SAS Literal

Word scanning continues.

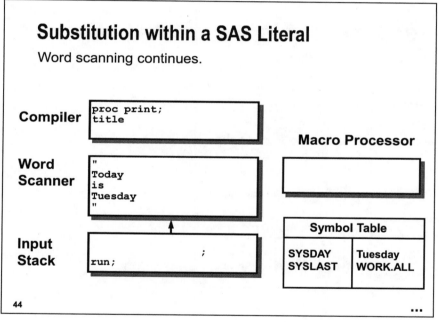

Substitution within a SAS Literal

The double-quoted literal is passed to the compiler as a unit.

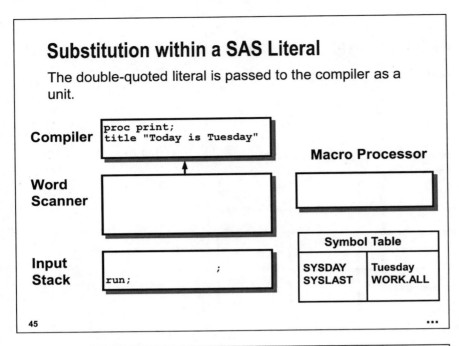

Compiler

```
proc print;
title "Today is Tuesday"
```

Word Scanner

Macro Processor

Input Stack

```
                              ;
run;
```

Symbol Table	
SYSDAY	Tuesday
SYSLAST	WORK.ALL

45   •••

Substitution within a SAS Literal

When a step boundary is encountered, compilation ends and execution begins.

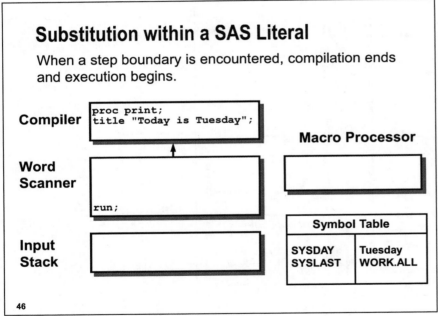

Compiler

```
proc print;
title "Today is Tuesday";
```

Word Scanner

Macro Processor

```
run;
```

Input Stack

Symbol Table	
SYSDAY	Tuesday
SYSLAST	WORK.ALL

46

2.04 Multiple Choice Poll

Macro variable references are resolved by which of the following?

a. SAS compiler
b. Macro processor
c. Word scanner

48

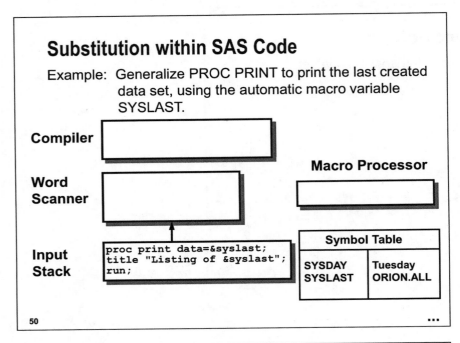

Substitution within SAS Code

Example: Generalize PROC PRINT to print the last created
data set, using the automatic macro variable
SYSLAST.

Compiler

Macro Processor

**Word
Scanner**

**Input
Stack**

```
proc print data=&syslast;
title "Listing of &syslast";
run;
```

Symbol Table	
SYSDAY	Tuesday
SYSLAST	ORION.ALL

50   ...

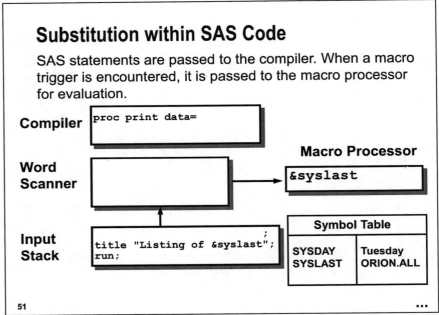

Substitution within SAS Code

SAS statements are passed to the compiler. When a macro
trigger is encountered, it is passed to the macro processor
for evaluation.

Compiler   `proc print data=`

Macro Processor

**Word
Scanner**   `&syslast`

**Input
Stack**
```
                           ;
title "Listing of &syslast";
run;
```

Symbol Table	
SYSDAY	Tuesday
SYSLAST	ORION.ALL

51   ...

Substitution within SAS Code

The *macro variable reference* triggers the macro processor to search the symbol table for the reference.

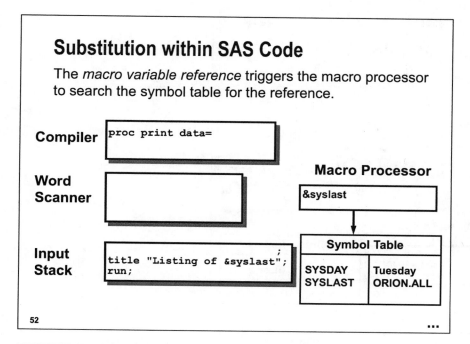

Substitution within SAS Code

The macro processor resolves the macro variable reference, passing its resolved value back to the input stack.

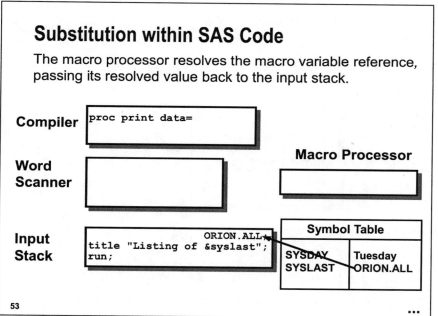

Substitution within SAS Code

Word scanning continues.

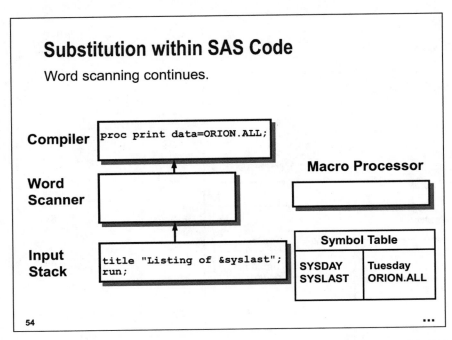

Substitution within SAS Code

A step boundary is encountered. Compilation ends.
Execution begins.

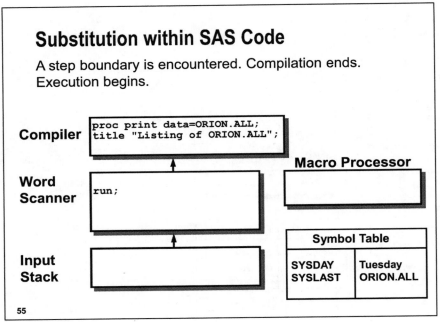

Unresolved Reference

Example: Reference a nonexistent macro variable within a SAS literal.

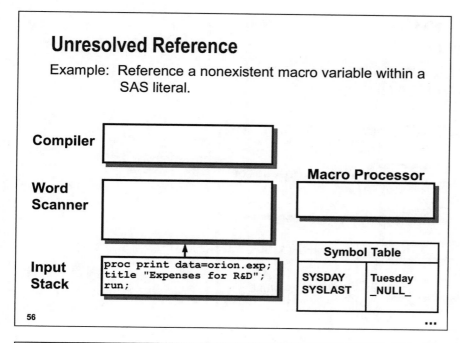

Compiler

Word Scanner

Macro Processor

Input Stack

```
proc print data=orion.exp;
title "Expenses for R&D";
run;
```

Symbol Table	
SYSDAY	Tuesday
SYSLAST	_NULL_

56

...

Unresolved Reference

The macro trigger is passed to the macro processor for evaluation.

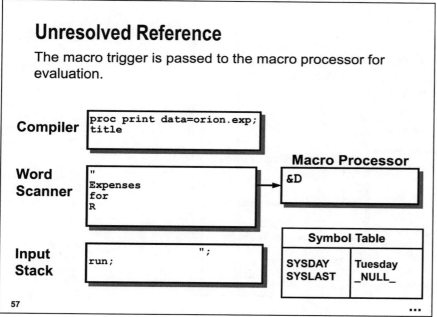

Compiler

```
proc print data=orion.exp;
title
```

Word Scanner

```
"
Expenses
for
R
```

Macro Processor

```
&D
```

Input Stack

```
                    ";
run;
```

Symbol Table	
SYSDAY	Tuesday
SYSLAST	_NULL_

57

...

Unresolved Reference

The macro processor writes a WARNING message to the
SAS log when it cannot resolve a reference.

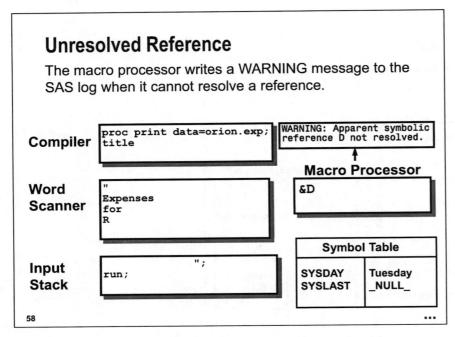

Unresolved Reference

If the macro processor cannot resolve a reference, the
tokens are passed back to the word scanner. The word
scanner passes them to the compiler.

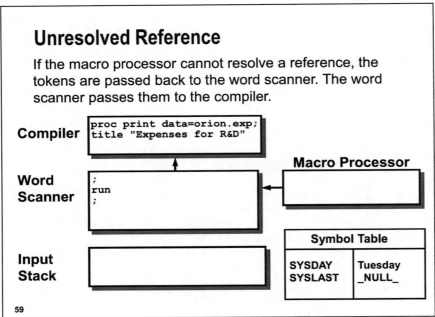

Unresolved Reference

Example: Reference a nonexistent macro variable within
SAS code.

```
proc print data=&sydlast;
title "Listing of &syslast";
run;
```

60

Unresolved Reference

SAS Log

```
1     proc print data=&sydlast;
                          -
                         22
                         200
WARNING: Apparent symbolic reference SYDLAST not resolved.
ERROR: File WORK.SYDLAST.DATA does not exist.
ERROR 22-322: Expecting a name.
ERROR 200-322: The symbol is not recognized and will be ignored.
2     title "Listing of &syslast";
3     run;

NOTE: The SAS System stopped processing this step because of errors.
NOTE: PROCEDURE PRINT used (Total process time):
      real time          0.65 seconds
      cpu time           0.09 seconds
```

61

Exercises

Submit a LIBNAME statement to assign the **orion** libref to the course SAS data library according to instructions provided by the instructor.

```
libname orion '_____';
```

Level 1

1. Displaying Automatic Macro Variables

a. Use the %PUT statement to list all automatic macro variables in the SAS log.

b. What are the values of the following automatic macro variables?

- SYSLAST _____
- SYSUSERID _____
- SYSTIME _____
- SYSDATE9 _____

c. Are the values for the automatic macro variables SYSTIME and SYSDATE9 accurate?

_____

_____

Level 2

2. Using Automatic Macro Variables

a. Using the SORT procedure, sort the data set **orion.continent** by **Continent_Name**.

> Use the OUT= option in the PROC SORT statement so that you do not overwrite the original data set.

b. Using the PRINT procedure and an automatic macro variable, print the most recently created data set and display the data set name in the title.

c. Submit the program and examine the results.

3. Using Automatic Macro Variables

a. What is the value of the automatic macro variable SYSLAST after the following DATA step is submitted? _____

```
data new;
   set orion.continent;
run;
```

b. What is the value of the automatic macro variable SYSLAST after the following PROC PRINT step is submitted?

_____

```
proc print data=orion.continent;
run;
```

Level 3

4. Using SAS Date Constants

a. Open the **m102e04** program shown below into the Editor window.

```
proc print data=orion.employee_payroll;
   format Birth_Date Employee_Hire_Date date9.;
run;
```

b. Modify the program so that it subsets the data to return only the employees hired between January 1, 2007, and today. Use the automatic macro variable SYSDATE9 to return today's date.

PROC PRINT Output

Obs	Employee_ID	Employee_ Gender	Salary	Birth_ Date	Employee_ Hire_Date	Employee_ Term_Date	Marital_ Status	Dependents
310	121034	M	27110	23AUG1988	01JAN2007	.	S	0
361	121085	M	32235	12NOV1986	01JAN2007	.	S	0
364	121088	M	27240	10JUN1988	01JAN2007	.	S	0

2.4   User-Defined Macro Variables

Objectives

- Create user-defined macro variables.
- Display values of user-defined macro variables
  in the SAS log.

65

The %LET Statement

The %LET statement creates a macro variable and assigns it a value.

General form of the %LET statement:

> **%LET** *variable=value*;

- *variable* follows SAS naming conventions.
- If *variable* already exists, its *value* is overwritten.
- If *variable* or *value* contain macro triggers, the triggers are evaluated before the %LET statement is executed.

%LET statements are valid in open code (anywhere in a SAS program).

66

The %LET Statement

Value can be any string:

- The maximum length is 65,534 (64K) characters.
- The minimum length is 0 characters (*null value*).
- Numeric tokens are stored as character strings.
- Mathematical expressions are **not** evaluated.
- The case of *value* is preserved.
- Quotation marks are stored as part of *value*.
- Leading and trailing blanks **are removed** from *value* before the assignment is made.

67

%LET Statement Examples

Determine the value assigned to each macro variable
by these %LET statements.

```
%let name= Ed Norton ;
%let name2=' Ed Norton ';
%let title="Joan's Report";
%let start=;
%let sum=3+4;
%let total=0;
%let total=&total+&sum;
%let x=varlist;
%let &x=name age height;
```

Global Symbol Table	

68   ...

%LET Statement Examples

The %LET statement truncates leading and trailing blanks.

```
%let name= Ed Norton ;
%let name2=' Ed Norton ';
%let title="Joan's Report";
%let start=;
%let sum=3+4;
%let total=0;
%let total=&total+&sum;
%let x=varlist;
%let &x=name age height;
```

Global Symbol Table	
name	Ed Norton

69   ...

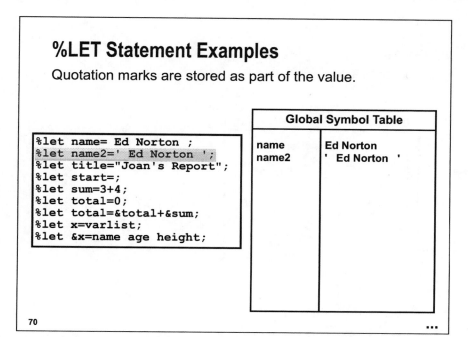

Storing quotation marks as part of a macro variable's value is **not** recommended.

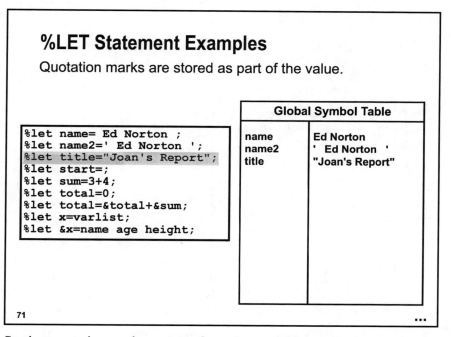

Storing quotation marks as part of a macro variable's value is **not** recommended.

%LET Statement Examples

A null value is stored.

```
%let name= Ed Norton ;
%let name2=' Ed Norton ';
%let title="Joan's Report";
%let start=;
%let sum=3+4;
%let total=0;
%let total=&total+&sum;
%let x=varlist;
%let &x=name age height;
```

Global Symbol Table	
name	Ed Norton
name2	' Ed Norton '
title	"Joan's Report"
start	

72   ...

%LET Statement Examples

Mathematical expressions are not evaluated.

```
%let name= Ed Norton ;
%let name2=' Ed Norton ';
%let title="Joan's Report";
%let start=;
%let sum=3+4;
%let total=0;
%let total=&total+&sum;
%let x=varlist;
%let &x=name age height;
```

Global Symbol Table	
name	Ed Norton
name2	' Ed Norton '
title	"Joan's Report"
start	
sum	3+4

73   ...

%LET Statement Examples

Numeric tokens are stored as character strings.

```
%let name= Ed Norton ;
%let name2=' Ed Norton ';
%let title="Joan's Report";
%let start=;
%let sum=3+4;
%let total=0;
%let total=&total+&sum;
%let x=varlist;
%let &x=name age height;
```

Global Symbol Table	
name	Ed Norton
name2	' Ed Norton '
title	"Joan's Report"
start	
sum	3+4
total	0

74 ...

%LET Statement Examples

The macro trigger is evaluated before the %LET statement executes. The previous value of TOTAL is replaced.

```
%let name= Ed Norton ;
%let name2=' Ed Norton ';
%let title="Joan's Report";
%let start=;
%let sum=3+4;
%let total=0;
%let total=&total+&sum;
%let x=varlist;
%let &x=name age height;
```

Global Symbol Table	
name	Ed Norton
name2	' Ed Norton '
title	"Joan's Report"
start	
sum	3+4
total	0+3+4

75 ...

%LET Statement Examples

```
%let name= Ed Norton ;
%let name2=' Ed Norton ';
%let title="Joan's Report";
%let start=;
%let sum=3+4;
%let total=0;
%let total=&total+&sum;
%let x=varlist;
%let &x=name age height;
```

Global Symbol Table	
name	Ed Norton
name2	' Ed Norton '
title	"Joan's Report"
start	
sum	3+4
total	0+3+4
x	varlist

76   ...

%LET Statement Examples

The macro variable's name resolves to **varlist**.

```
%let name= Ed Norton ;
%let name2=' Ed Norton ';
%let title="Joan's Report";
%let start=;
%let sum=3+4;
%let total=0;
%let total=&total+&sum;
%let x=varlist;
%let &x=name age height;
```

Global Symbol Table	
name	Ed Norton
name2	' Ed Norton '
title	"Joan's Report"
start	
sum	3+4
total	0+3+4
x	varlist
varlist	name age height

77

2.05 Quiz

Macro variables store numeric tokens as ...?

79

%LET Statement Examples

Example: Use a macro variable to select a **numeric value**.

```
%let units=4;
proc print data=orion.Order_Fact;
   where Quantity > &units;
   var Order_Date Product_ID Quantity;
   title "Orders exceeding &units units";
run;
```

Macro variables store numbers as text, not as numeric values.

m102d02

81

%LET Statement Examples

SAS Log

```
1    %let units=4;
2    proc print data=orion.Order_Fact;
3       where Quantity > &units;
4       var Order_Date Product_ID Quantity;
5       title "Orders exceeding &units units";
6    run;

NOTE: There were 6 observations read from the data set ORION.ORDER_FACT.
      WHERE Quantity>4;
NOTE: PROCEDURE PRINT used (Total process time):
      real time           0.70 seconds
      cpu time            0.15 seconds
```

82

%LET Statement Examples

Example: Use a macro variable to select a **character value**.

```
%let office=Sydney;
proc print data=orion.Employee_Addresses;
   where City="&office";
   var Employee_Name;
   title "&office Employees";
run;
```

83   m102d03

%LET Statement Examples

SAS Log

```
55   %let office=Sydney;
56   proc print data=orion.Employee_Addresses;
57      where City="&office";
58      var Employee_Name;
59      title "&office Employees";
60   run;

NOTE: There were 67 observations read from the data set ORION.EMPLOYEE_ADDRESSES.
      WHERE City='Sydney';
NOTE: PROCEDURE PRINT used (Total process time):
      real time           0.00 seconds
      cpu time            0.00 seconds
```

84

SAS Programming Review

Character constants are enclosed in quotation marks.

where City="&office"; ← **right**
   resolves to ....
where City="Sydney"; ← **right**

where City='&office'; ← **wrong**
   resolves to ....
where City='&office'; ← **wrong**

where City=&office; ← **wrong**
   resolves to ....
where City=Sydney; ← **wrong**

85

%LET Statement Examples

Example: Use macro variables to select dates.

```
%let date1=25may2007;
%let date2=15jun2007;
proc print data=orion.Order_Fact;
   where Order_Date between "&date1"d and "&date2"d;
   var Order_Date Product_ID Quantity;
   title "Orders between &date1 and &date2";
run;
```

86   m102d04

%LET Statement Examples

SAS Log

```
61    %let date1=25may2007;
62    %let date2=15jun2007;
63    proc print data=orion.Order_Fact;
64       where Order_Date between "&date1"d and "&date2"d;
65       var Order_Date Product_ID Quantity;
66       title "Orders between &date1 and &date2";
67    run;
NOTE: There were 11 observations read from the data set ORION.ORDER_FACT.
      WHERE (Order_Date>='25MAY2007'D and Order_Date<='15JUN2007'D);
NOTE: PROCEDURE PRINT used (Total process time):
      real time           0.00 seconds
      cpu time            0.00 seconds
```

87

%LET Statement Examples

PROC PRINT Output

```
       Orders between 25may2007 and 15jun2007

            Order_
 Obs         Date      Product_ID      Quantity

 526       05JUN2007   240100100679       2
 527       06JUN2007   230100400007       1
 528       07JUN2007   240100100690       2
 529       07JUN2007   240100100737       5
 530       08JUN2007   220200200036       2
 531       08JUN2007   220200200077       2
 532       10JUN2007   220200100009       2
 533       11JUN2007   230100500056       2
 534       11JUN2007   230100500087       2
 535       13JUN2007   240200100057       4
 536       15JUN2007   240200100118       4
```

88

2.06 Quiz

How should the WHERE statement be written in the program below?

Hint: Be sure to use the CITY and SALARY macro variables.

```
%let City=New York;
%let Salary=50000;
data work.a;
   set work.b;
   where city=          and salary gt          ;
run;
```

90

Displaying Macro Variables

Example: Display all user-defined macro variables in the SAS log.

```
%put _user_;
```

Partial SAS Log

```
175  %put _user_;
GLOBAL OFFICE Sydney
GLOBAL DATE1 25may2007
GLOBAL DATE2 15jun2007
GLOBAL UNITS 4
```

92

Use _ALL_ to display all user-defined and automatic macro variables in the SAS log, as follows:

```
%put _all_;
```

Displaying Macro Variables

The SYMBOLGEN system option writes macro variable values to the SAS log as they are resolved.

General form of the SYMBOLGEN system option:

OPTIONS SYMBOLGEN;

✏ The default option is NOSYMBOLGEN.

93

Displaying Macro Variables

Partial SAS Log

```
176  options symbolgen;
177  %let office=Sydney;
178  proc print data=orion.employee_addresses;
179    where city="&office";
SYMBOLGEN:  Macro variable OFFICE resolves to Sydney
180    var employee_name;
SYMBOLGEN:  Macro variable OFFICE resolves to Sydney
181    title "&office Employees";
182  run;
```

✏ The location of SYMBOLGEN messages in the log is determined by SAS.

94

After debugging, issue the following statement to turn off the SYMBOLGEN option:

```
options nosymbolgen;
```

Deleting User-Defined Macro Variables

The %SYMDEL statement deletes one or more user-defined macro variables from the global symbol table.

To release memory, delete macro variables from the global symbol table when they are no longer needed.

General form of the %SYMDEL statement:

%SYMDEL *macro-variables*;

Example: Delete the macro variables OFFICE and UNITS.

```
%symdel office units;
```

95

 **Exercises**

Level 1

5. **Defining and Using Macro Variables for Character Substitution**

   a. Open the **m102e05** program shown below into the Editor window. Submit the program and examine the output that it creates.

   ```
   proc print data=orion.customer_dim;
      var Customer_Name Customer_Gender Customer_Age;
      where Customer_Group contains 'Gold';
      title 'Gold Customers';
   run
   ```

   b. Modify the program so that the two occurrences of Gold are replaced by references to the macro variable TYPE. Precede the program with a %LET statement to assign the value Gold to TYPE. Submit the program. It produces the same output as before.

   c. Include the appropriate system option to display resolved values of macro variables in the SAS log. Resubmit the program and examine the log.

   d. Modify the value of TYPE to Internet. Resubmit the program and examine the log.

   e. Turn off the system option from part **c** above.

Level 2

6. Defining and Using Macro Variables for Numeric Substitution

   a. Open the **m102e06** program shown below into the Editor window. Edit the program to display only the Gold level customers between the ages of 30 to 45.

     ✎   Customer ages range from 19 to 73.

```
%let type=Gold;
proc print data=orion.customer_dim;
    var Customer_Name Customer_Gender Customer_Age;
    where Customer_Group contains "&type";
    title "&type Customers";
run;
```

SAS Output

```
                          Gold Customers between 30 and 45

                                             Customer_      Customer_
                   Obs     Customer_Name       Gender          Age

                    3     Cornelia Krahl          F             33
                   11     Oliver S. Füßling       M             43
                   32     James Klisurich         M             38
                   35     Viola Folsom            F             38
                   40     Kyndal Hooks            F             43
                   57     Rita Lotz               F             43
                   75     Angel Borwick           F             38
```

   b. Modify the program so that the values 30 and 45 are replaced by references to the macro variables AGE1 and AGE2, respectively.

   c. Include the appropriate system option to display resolved values of macro variables in the SAS log. Resubmit the program and examine the log.

   d. Modify the values of AGE1 and AGE2. Resubmit the program and examine the log.

   e. Turn off the system option from part **c** above.

7. Deleting Macro Variables

   a. Open the program **m102e07** program shown below into the Editor window. Submit the program to create the macro variables.

```
%let pet1=Paisley;
%let pet2=Sitka;
```

   b. Delete all user-defined macro variables.

   c. Use the %PUT statement to verify that the macro variable deletion was successful.

2.5   Delimiting Macro Variable References

Objectives

- Place a macro variable reference adjacent to text or another macro variable reference.

99

Referencing Macro Variables

You can reference macro variables anywhere in your program, including these special situations:

Macro variable references adjacent to leading and/or trailing text:

> **text**&*variable*
> &*variable***text**
> **text**&*variable***text**

Adjacent macro variable references:

> &*variable*&*variable*

100

Combining Macro Variables with Text

You can place text immediately before a macro variable reference to build a new token.

Example: Data sets are stored in a SAS data library with a naming convention of **Y**yyyymon.

yyyy   can be **2000**, **2001**, **2002**, and so on.

mon   can be **JAN**, **FEB**, **MAR**, and so on.

Write an application that uses macro variables to build SAS data set names and other tokens.

101

Combining Macro Variables with Text

```
%let month=jan;
proc chart data=orion.y2000&month;
   hbar week / sumvar=sale;
run;
proc plot data=orion.y2000&month;
   plot sale*day;
run;
```

generates

```
proc chart data=orion.y2000jan;
   hbar week / sumvar=sale;
run;
proc plot data=orion.y2000jan;
   plot sale*day;
run;
```

102

Combining Macro Variables with Text

This example illustrates adjacent macro variable references.

Example: Modify the previous program to allow both the **month** and the **year** to be substituted.

```
%let year=2000;
%let month=jan;
proc chart data=orion.y&year&month;
   hbar week / sumvar=sale;
run;
proc plot data=orion.y&year&month;
   plot sale*day;
run;
```

103

Combining Macro Variables with Text

The generated program is identical to the program in the previous example.

```
proc chart data=orion.y2000jan;
   hbar week / sumvar=sale;
run;
proc plot data=orion.y2000jan;
   plot sale*day;
run;
```

104

Combining Macro Variables with Text

You can place text immediately after a macro variable reference if it does not change the reference.

Example: Modify the previous program to substitute the name of an analysis variable.

```
%let year=2000;
%let month=jan;
%let var=sale;
proc chart data=orion.y&year&month;
   hbar week / sumvar=&var;
run;
proc plot data=orion.y&year&month;
   plot &var*day;
run;
```

105

Combining Macro Variables with Text

The generated program is identical to the program in the previous example.

```
proc chart data=orion.y2000jan;
hbar week / sumvar=sale;
run;
proc plot data=orion.y2000jan;
plot sale*day;
run;
```

106

2.07 Quiz

Modify the previous program to allow a Base SAS or SAS/GRAPH procedure.

```
/* GRAPHICS should be null or G */
%let graphics=g;
%let year=2000;
%let month=jan;
%let var=sale;
proc &graphicschart data=orion.y&year&month;
   hbar week / sumvar=&var;
run;
proc &graphicsplot data=orion.y&year&month;
   plot &var*day;
run;
```

What is the problem with this reference?

108

Macro Variable Name Delimiter

The word scanner recognizes the end of a macro variable reference when it encounters a character that cannot be part of the reference.

A *period* (.) is a special delimiter that ends a macro variable reference. The period does not appear as text when the macro variable is resolved.

110

Macro Variable Name Delimiter

Example: Correct the problem from the previous example.

```
%let graphics=g;
%let year=2000;
%let month=jan;
%let var=sale;
proc &graphics.chart data=orion.y&year&month;
   hbar week / sumvar=&var;
run;
proc &graphics.plot data=orion.y&year&month;
   plot &var*day;
run;
```

111

Macro Variable Name Delimiter

The generated code does not include the period.

```
proc gchart data=orion.y2000jan;
   hbar week / sumvar=sale;
run;
proc gplot data=orion.y2000jan;
   plot sale*day;
run;
```

112

2.08 Quiz

Modify the previous example to include a macro variable that stores a libref.

```
%let lib=orion;
%let graphics=g;
%let year=2000;
%let month=jan;
%let var=sale;
libname &lib 'SAS-data-library';
proc &graphics.chart data=&lib.y&year&month;
   hbar week / sumvar=&var;
run;
proc &graphics.plot data=&lib.y&year&month;
   plot &var*day;
run;
```

How do these references resolve?

114

Macro Variable Name Delimiter

Use another period after the delimiter period to supply the needed token.

```
%let lib=orion;
...
libname &lib 'SAS-data-library';
proc &graphics.chart data=&lib..y&year&month;
...
proc &graphics.plot data=&lib..y&year&month;
```

116

Macro Variable Name Delimiter

delimiter ──────────┐ ┌────────── text

```
proc &graphics.chart data=&lib..y&year&month;
```

The first period is treated as a delimiter, the second
as text.

The compiler receives this:

```
...
proc gchart data=orion.y2000jan;
...
```

117

Exercises

Level 1

8. Consecutive Macro Variable References

   a. Open the **m102e08** program shown below into the Editor window. Submit the program and examine the output that it creates.

```
proc print data=orion.organization_dim;
   where Employee_Hire_Date='01AUG2006'd;
   id Employee_ID;
   var Employee_Name Employee_Country Employee_Hire_Date;
   title 'Personal Information for Employees Hired in AUG 2006';
run;
```

   b. Modify the program so that the two occurrences of AUG and 2006 are replaced by references to the macro variables MONTH and YEAR, respectively. Precede the program with %LET statements to assign the value AUG to MONTH and the value 2006 to YEAR. Submit the program. It produces the same output as before.

   c. Modify the value of MONTH to JUL and YEAR to 2003. Resubmit the program.

Level 2

9. Macro Variable References with Delimiters

   a. Open the **m102e09** program shown below into the Editor window. Submit the program and examine the output that it creates.

```
proc print data=orion.organization_dim;
   id Employee_ID;
   var Employee_Name Employee_Country Employee_Gender;
   title 'Listing of All Employees From Orion.Organization_Dim';
run;
```

   b. Modify the program so that all occurrences of Organization and Employee are replaced with macro variable references called DSN and VAR, respectively. Submit the program and verify the output.

   > When substituting for the hardcoded **Employees** in the TITLE statement, be sure to keep the ending **s** as part of the title text.

   c. Modify the value of DSN to Customer and VAR to Customer. Resubmit the program.

Level 3

10. Macro Variable References with Multiple Delimiters

a. Open the **m102e10** program shown below into the Editor window. This program analyzes the `orion.staff` data to find the employee with the most seniority within a job title. Submit the program and examine the output that it creates.

```
proc sort data=orion.staff out=staffhires;
   by Job_Title Emp_Hire_Date;
run;
data FirstHired;
   set staffhires;
   by Job_Title;
   if First.Job_Title;
run;
proc print data=FirstHired;
   id Job_Title;
   var Employee_ID Emp_Hire_Date;
   title "First Employee Hired within Each Job Title";
run;
```

b. Using a macro variable, modify the program to return the employees with the most or least amount of seniority. Be sure to make any necessary modifications to the title.

Partial PROC PRINT Output

First Employee Hired within Each Job Title		
Job_Title	Employee_ID	Emp_Hire_Date
Account Manager	120746	01APR2002
Accountant I	120752	01AUG1975
Accountant II	120771	01DEC1976
Accountant III	120757	01JAN1974
Administration Manager	120104	01JAN1981
Applications Developer I	120797	01DEC1977
Applications Developer II	120796	01MAR1983
Applications Developer IV	120802	01JAN1978

Partial PROC PRINT Output

Last Employee Hired within Each Job Title		
Job_Title	Employee_ID	Emp_Hire_Date
Account Manager	120746	01APR2002
Accountant I	120761	01JUL2006
Accountant II	120754	01MAY2006
Accountant III	120755	01AUG1983
Administration Manager	121000	01DEC1993
Applications Developer I	120801	01JUL1999
Applications Developer II	120812	01AUG2001
Applications Developer IV	120794	01JUL2003

2.6 Macro Functions

Objectives

- Use macro functions to do the following:
  - manipulate text
  - perform arithmetic operations
  - execute SAS functions

121

Macro Functions

The following are true for macro functions:

- have similar syntax as corresponding DATA step character functions
- yield similar results
- manipulate macro variables and expressions
- represent macro triggers
- are executed by the macro processor
- do not require quotation marks around character constant arguments

122

Macro Functions

Selected character string manipulation functions:

%UPCASE	translates letters from lowercase to uppercase.
%SUBSTR	extracts a substring from a character string.
%SCAN	extracts a word from a character string.
%INDEX	searches a character string for specified text.

Other functions:

%EVAL	performs arithmetic and logical operations.
%SYSFUNC	executes SAS functions.
%STR	quotes special characters.
%NRSTR	quotes special characters, including macro triggers.

123

Macro Functions

Arguments to macro string manipulation functions can be any text and/or macro triggers:

- constant text
- macro variable references
- macro functions
- macro calls

Constant text arguments do not require quotation marks.

124

Macro Functions

Example: Use macro functions to avoid hardcoding the
year and data set name highlighted below.

```
data orders;
   set orion.Orders;
   where year(Order_Date)= 2007;
   Lag=Delivery_Date - Order_Date;
run;

proc means data=orders maxdec=2 min max mean;
   class Order_Type;
   var Lag;
   title "Report based on ORDERS data";
run;
```

Symbol Table

```
SYSDATE9    23JAN2007
SYSLAST     WORK.ORDERS
```

m102d05a

125

The %SUBSTR Function

General form of the %SUBSTR function:

> **%SUBSTR**(*argument, position <,n>*)

- The %SUBSTR function returns the portion of *argument* beginning at *position* for a length of *n* characters.
- When *n* is not supplied, the %SUBSTR function returns the portion of *argument* beginning at *position* to the end of *argument*.

126

The values of *position* and *n* can also be the result of an arithmetic expression that yields an integer. For example,

```
%substr(&var,%length(&var)-1)
```

returns the last two characters of the value of the macro variable VAR.

The %SUBSTR Function

Example: Substring the year portion of SYSDATE9.

SAS Log

```
165  %put sysdate9=&sysdate9;
sysdate9=16JAN2008
166  %put year=%substr(&sysdate9,6);
year=2008
```

127

2.09 Multiple Choice Poll

What is the value of **X** after %LET statement execution?

```
%let X=%substr("ABCD",2,1);
```

a. Ⓐ
b. B
c. C
d. D

129

The %SCAN Function

General form of the %SCAN function:

> **%SCAN**(*argument, n <,delimiters>*)

The %SCAN function does the following:

- returns the *n*th word of *argument*, where words are strings of characters separated by delimiters
- uses a default set of delimiters if none are specified
- returns a null string if there are fewer than *n* words in *argument*

131

The following are default delimiters for the %SCAN function: **blank . (& ! $ *) ; - / , %**

It is not necessary to place *argument* and *delimiters* in quotation marks because they are always handled as character strings by the %SCAN function.

The %SCAN Function

Example: Scan SYSLAST for a one-level data set name.

SAS Log

```
41    %put syslast=&syslast;
syslast=WORK.ORDERS
42    %put dsn=%scan(&syslast,2,.);
dsn=ORDERS
```

132

Macro Functions

Step 1: Write and debug a program with hardcoded constants.

```
data orders;
   set orion.Orders;
   where year(Order_Date)=2007;
   Lag=Delivery_Date - Order_Date;
run;

proc means data=orders maxdec=2 min max mean;
   class Order_Type;
   var Lag;
   title "Report based on ORDERS data";
run;
```

m102d05a

133

Macro Functions

Step 2: Use macro functions to manipulate automatic macro variables for substitution within SAS code.

```
data orders;
   set orion.Orders;
   where year(Order_Date)=%substr(&sysdate9,6);
   Lag=Delivery_Date - Order_Date;
run;

proc means data=&syslast maxdec=2 min max mean;
   class Order_Type;
   var Lag;
   title "Report based on %scan(&syslast,2,.) data";
run;
```

m102d05b

134

Macro Functions

PROC MEANS Output

		Report based on ORDERS data		
		Analysis Variable : Lag		
Order Type	N Obs	Minimum	Maximum	Mean
1	70	0.00	10.00	0.43
2	15	2.00	10.00	4.27
3	31	1.00	7.00	3.87

135

The %EVAL Function

General form of the %EVAL function:

> **%EVAL**(*expression*)

The %EVAL function does the following:
- performs arithmetic and logical operations
- truncates non-integer results
- returns a text result
- returns 1 (true) or 0 (false) for logical operations
- returns a null value and issues an error message when non-integer values are used in arithmetic operations

136

The %EVAL Function

Example: Perform simple integer arithmetic.

```
%let x=%eval(2+2);
%put x=&x;
```

SAS Log

```
154   %let x=%eval(2+2);
155   %put x=&x;
x=4
```

137

The %EVAL Function

Example: Compute the first year of a range based on the current date.

```
%let thisyr=%substr(&sysdate9,6);
%let lastyr=%eval(&thisyr-1);
proc means data=orion.order_fact maxdec=2 min max mean;
   class order_type;
   var total_retail_price;
   where year(order_date) between &lastyr and &thisyr;
   title1 "Orders for &lastyr and &thisyr";
   title2 "(as of &sysdate9)";
run;
```

m102d06

The %EVAL Function

PROC MEANS Output

```
                        Orders for 2007 and 2008
                           (as of 24JAN2008)

                          The MEANS Procedure

   Analysis Variable : Total_Retail_Price Total Retail Price for This Product

                        N
        Order Type     Obs      Minimum        Maximum          Mean

                 1      89          3.20       1066.40         122.01

                 2      19          8.20       1937.20         301.01

                 3      40          9.60        702.00         168.28
```

The %SYSFUNC Function

The %SYSFUNC macro function executes SAS functions.

General form of the %SYSFUNC function:

> **%SYSFUNC***(SAS function(argument(s)) <,format>)*

- *SAS function(argument(s))* is the name of a SAS function and its corresponding arguments.
- The second argument is an optional format for the value returned by the first argument.

140

The %SYSFUNC Function

Example:

```
%put syslast=&syslast;
%let dsn=%sysfunc(propcase(&syslast));
%put dsn=&dsn;
```

SAS Log

```
156  %put syslast=&syslast;
syslast=WORK.ORDERS
157  %let dsn=%sysfunc(propcase(&syslast));
158  %put dsn=&dsn;
dsn=Work.Orders
```

The PROPCASE function converts text to proper case.

141

The %SYSFUNC Function

The automatic macro variables SYSDATE9 and SYSTIME can be used in titles.

```
title1 "&sysdate9";
title2 "&systime";
```

generates

```
07MAR2008
   13:39
```

SYSDATE9 and SYSTIME represent the **date** and **time** that the SAS session began.

142

m102d07

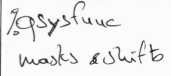

The %SYSFUNC Function

Example: Generate titles that contain the current date and time, appropriately formatted.

```
title1 "%sysfunc(today(),weekdate.)";
title2 "%sysfunc(time(),timeAMPM8.)";
```

generates

```
Monday, March 10, 2008
        4:27 PM
```

143

m102d07

The %SYSFUNC Function

Most SAS functions can be used with %SYSFUNC.
Exceptions include the following:

- array processing (DIM, HBOUND, LBOUND)
- variable information (VNAME, VLABEL, MISSING)
- macro interface (RESOLVE, SYMGET)
- data conversion (INPUT, PUT)
- other functions (IORCMSG, LAG, DIF)

✎ INPUTC and INPUTN can be used in place of INPUT.
     PUTC and PUTN can be used in place of PUT.

144

✎   Variable information functions are functions such as VNAME and VLABEL. For a complete list,
      see "Functions and CALL Routines" in *SAS® Language Reference: Dictionary*.

✎   Because %SYSFUNC is a macro function, you do not need to enclose character values in
      quotation marks as you do in DATA step functions. Use commas to separate all arguments
      in DATA step functions within %SYSFUNC. You cannot use argument lists that are preceded
      by the word OF.

2.10 Multiple Answer Poll

You can use macro functions to do which of the following:

a. Manipulate text
b. Execute SAS functions
c. Manipulate SAS data set variables
d. Perform arithmetic

146

2.11 Quiz

Submit program **m102a01**.

```
%let statement=title "Payroll Report";
%put &statement;
```

What is the value of STATEMENT?

What is the potential problem with the value of STATEMENT?

149

The %STR Function

The %STR function masks (removes the normal meaning of) these special tokens:

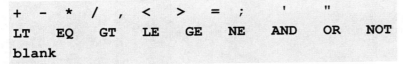

```
+   -   *   /   ,   <   >   =   ;       '       "
LT   EQ   GT   LE   GE   NE   AND   OR   NOT
blank
```

General form of the %STR function:

%STR(*argument*)

argument   can be any combination of text and macro triggers.

151

The %STR Function

The following are true for the %STR function:
- masks tokens, so the macro processor does not interpret them as macro-level syntax
- enables macro triggers to work normally
- preserves leading and trailing blanks in its argument
- masks an unpaired quotation mark or parenthesis in its argument when the quotation mark or parenthesis is immediately preceded by a percent sign (%)

152

The %STR function does not mask & and % characters.

The %STR Function

Example: Store a SAS statement in a macro variable.

```
%let statement=%str(title "S&P 500";);
```

SAS Log

```
3    %let statement=%str(title 'S&P 500';);
WARNING: Apparent symbolic reference P not resolved.
```

153   m102d08

% bquote masks
     what SAS types
% str masks what
     you type

The %NRSTR Function

The %NRSTR function works the same as the %STR
function, except that it also masks macro triggers.

Example: Use %NRSTR to prevent attempted macro
variable resolution.

```
%let statement=%nrstr(title "S&P 500";);
```

154

In addition to %STR and %NRSTR, several other macro quoting functions are available for specialized purposes. For further information, see *Macro Quoting* under *Understanding and Using the Macro Facility* under *SAS Macro Reference* in Base SAS documentation.

 **Exercises**

Level 1

11. Using the %SUBSTR and %SCAN Functions

    a. Submit a %LET statement to assign the value `Anthony Miller` to a macro variable named FULLNAME.

    b. Extract the first initial and last name, putting them together into a new macro variable as `A. Miller`. Use the %PUT statement to display the results.

12. Using the %SYSFUNC Function

    Use the %PUT statement and the %SYSFUNC function to display the current date and time. Format the date with the MMDDYYP10. format and the time with TIMEAMPM. format.

Level 2

13. Using Macro Functions

    a. Open the **m102e13** program shown below into the Editor window. Submit the program and examine the output that it creates. Verify the titles.

```
%let d=&sysdate9;
%let t=&systime;
proc print data=orion.product_dim;
   where Product_Name contains "Jacket";
   var Product_Name Product_ID Supplier_Name;
   title1 "Product Names Containing 'Jacket'";
   title2 "Report produced &t &d";
run;
```

    b. Submit a %LET statement to assign the value `R&D` to a macro variable named PRODUCT. Reference the new macro variable in the WHERE statement and the TITLE1 statement. Submit the modified program.

    PROC PRINT Output

```
                     Product Names Containing 'R&D'
                       Report produced 14:06 17FEB2009


        Obs    Product_Name                  Product_ID    Supplier_Name

        393    Top Men's R&D Ultimate Jacket 240300300070  Top Sports Inc
        395    Top R&D Long Jacket           240300300090  Top Sports Inc
```

Level 3

14. **Manipulating Macro Variables**

   a. Assign your birth date to a macro variable.

   b. Issue a %PUT statement that writes the day of the week that you were born.

2.7 Chapter Review

Chapter Review

1. Where are macro variables stored?

2. What are the two kinds of macro variables?

3. What is the maximum length of a macro variable?

4. How do you reference a macro variable?

157

Chapter Review

5. What macro language statement creates macro variables?

6. How can you view all user-defined macro variables?

7. What SAS option displays macro variable values as they are resolved?

8. What macro language function executes SAS functions?

159

2.8 Solutions

Solutions to Exercises

1. **Displaying Automatic Macro Variables**

   a. The _AUTOMATIC_ argument in the %PUT statement displays the values of all automatic macro variables in the SAS log. Many of the values shown are dependent on the host system.

   ```
   %put _automatic_ ;
   ```

   b. The value of SYSLAST will be _NULL_ unless a data set has been created. Then it would be the name of the last created data set. The value of SYSUSERID is dependent on the host system. The value of SYSTIME and SYSDATE9 will be the initialization time of your SAS session.

   c. The values of SYSTIME and SYSDATE do not reflect the current time and date; instead, they reflect the initialization time of the SAS session. Therefore, the values are not always accurate.

2. **Using Automatic Macro Variables**

   a. Using the SORT procedure, sort the data set **orion.continent** by **Continent_Name**.

   ```
   proc sort data=orion.continent out=sorted;
      by Continent_Name;
   run;
   ```

   b. The SYSLAST automatic macro variable contains the name of the most recently created data set.

   ```
   proc print data=&syslast;
      title "&syslast";
   run;
   ```

   c. Submit the program and examine the results.

   SAS Output

   ```
                         WORK.SORTED

                      Continent_
           Obs          ID        Continent_Name

            1           94        Africa
            2           95        Asia
            3           96        Australia/Pacific
            4           93        Europe
            5           91        North America
   ```

3. Using Automatic Macro Variables

a. The DATA step would alter the value of SYSLAST to `WORK.NEW`.

```
data new;
   set orion.continent;
run;
```

b. The value of SYSLAST is still `WORK.NEW`. The PRINT procedure does not create a SAS data set; therefore, it does not alter the value of SYSLAST.

```
proc print data=orion.continent;
run;
```

4. Using SAS Data Constants

a. Open the program into the Editor window.

b. Modify the program so that it subsets the data to return only the employees hired between January 1, 2007, and today. Use the automatic macro variable SYSDATE9 to return today's date.

```
proc print data=orion.employee_payroll;
   format Birth_Date Employee_Hire_Date date9.;
   where Employee_Hire_Date between '01jan2007'd and "&sysdate"d;
run;
```

5. Defining and Using Macro Variables for Character Substitution

a. Submit the program below.

```
proc print data=orion.customer_dim;
   var Customer_Name Customer_Gender Customer_Age;
   where Customer_Group contains "Gold";
   title "Gold Customers";
run;
```

Partial SAS Output

```
                          Gold Customers

                        Customer_    Customer_
       Obs  Customer_Name    Gender       Age

         2  Sandrina Stephano    F          24
         3  Cornelia Krahl       F          29
         7  Markus Sepke         M          15
        11  Oliver S. Füßling    M          39
```

b. The macro variable TYPE should contain the text string `Gold` without any surrounding quotation marks. To resolve the macro variable in the WHERE and TITLE statements, change the single quotation marks to double quotation marks. It produces the same output as before.

```
%let type=Gold;
proc print data=orion.customer_dim;
   var Customer_Name Customer_Gender Customer_Age;
   where Customer_Group contains "&type";
   title "&type Customers";
run;
```

c. Turn on the SYMBOLGEN option.

```
option symbolgen;
%let type=Gold;
proc print data=orion.customer_dim;
   var Customer_Name Customer_Gender Customer_Age;
   where Customer_Group contains "&type";
   title "&type Customers";
run;
```

Partial SAS Log

```
79    proc print data=orion.customer_dim;
80        var customer_name customer_gender customer_age;
81        where customer_group contains "&type";
SYMBOLGEN:  Macro variable TYPE resolves to Gold
SYMBOLGEN:  Macro variable TYPE resolves to Gold
82        title "&type Customers";
83    run;
```

d. Modify the value of TYPE to `Internet`.

```
%let type=Internet;
proc print data=orion.customer_dim;
   var Customer_name Customer_Gender Customer_age;
   where Customer_Group contains "&type";
   title "&type Customers";
run;
```

Partial SAS Log

```
63    %let type=Internet;
64    proc print data=orion.customer_dim;
65        var customer_name customer_gender customer_age;
66        where customer_group contains "&type";
SYMBOLGEN:  Macro variable TYPE resolves to Internet
SYMBOLGEN:  Macro variable TYPE resolves to Internet
67        title "&type Customers";
68    run;

NOTE: There were 8 observations read from the data set ORION.CUSTOMER_DIM.
      WHERE customer_group contains 'Internet';
NOTE: PROCEDURE PRINT used (Total process time):
      real time           5.04 seconds
      cpu time            0.01 seconds
```

e. Turn off the SYMBOLGEN option.

```
option nosymbolgen;
```

6. Defining and Using Macro Variables for Numeric Substitution

a. Edit the program to also subset the data for customers between the ages of 30 and 45.

```
%let type=Gold;
proc print data=orion.customer_dim;
   var Customer_Name Customer_Gender Customer_Age;
   where Customer_Group contains "&type" and
         Customer_Age between 30 and 45;
   title "&type Customers between 30 and 45";
run;
```

b. Modify the program so that the values 30 and 45 are replaced by references to the macro variables AGE1 and AGE2, respectively.

```
%let type=Gold;
%let age1=30;
%let age2=45;
proc print data=orion.customer_dim;
   var Customer_Name Customer_Gender Customer_Age;
   where Customer_Group contains "&type" and
         Customer_Age between &age1 and &age2 ;
   title "&type Customers between &age1 and &age2";
run;
```

c. Include the appropriate system option to display resolved values of macro variables in the SAS log. Resubmit the program and examine the log.

```
options symbolgen;
```

d. Modify the value of AGE1 and AGE2. Resubmit the program and examine the log.

Partial SAS Log

```
88   %let type=Gold;
89   %let age1=20;
90   %let age2=30;
91   proc print data=orion.customer_dim;
92      var customer_name customer_gender customer_age;
93      where customer_group contains "&type" and Customer_Age between &age1 and &age2 ;
SYMBOLGEN:  Macro variable TYPE resolves to Gold
SYMBOLGEN:  Macro variable AGE1 resolves to 20
SYMBOLGEN:  Macro variable AGE2 resolves to 30
SYMBOLGEN:  Macro variable TYPE resolves to Gold
SYMBOLGEN:  Macro variable AGE1 resolves to 20
SYMBOLGEN:  Macro variable AGE2 resolves to 30
94      title "&type Customers between &age1 and &age2";
95   run;

NOTE: There were 7 observations read from the data set ORION.CUSTOMER_DIM.
      WHERE customer_group contains 'Gold' and (Customer_Age>=20 and Customer_Age<=30);
```

e. Turn off the SYMBOLGEN option.

```
options nosymbolgen;
```

7. Deleting Macro Variables

a. Open the program and submit the code. _USER_ will list all user-defined macro variables in the SAS log.

```
%put _user_;
```

b. The %SYMDEL statement deletes user-defined macro variables.

```
%symdel type age1 age2 pet1 pet2;
```

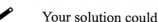 Your solution could be different. It depends on the macro variables created during the current SAS session.

c. Use the %PUT statement to verify that the macro variable deletion was successful.

```
%put _user_;
```

8. Consecutive Macro Variable References

a. Open the program into the Editor window.

b. Modify the program so that the two occurrences of AUG and 2006 are replaced by references to the macro variables MONTH and YEAR, respectively.

```
%let month=AUG;
%let year=2006;
proc print data=orion.organization_dim;
   where Employee_Hire_Date="01&month&year"d;
   id Employee_ID;
   var Employee_Name Employee_Country Employee_Hire_Date;
   title "Personal Information for Employees Hired in "
         "&month &year";
run;
```

c. Modify the value of MONTH to JUL and YEAR to 2003. Resubmit the program.

```
%let month=JUL;
%let year=2003;
proc print data=orion.organization_dim;
   where Employee_Hire_Date="01&month&year"d;
   id Employee_ID;
   var Employee_Name Employee_Country Employee_Hire_Date;
   title "Personal Information for Employees Hired in "
         "&month &year";
run;
```

9. Macro Variable References with Delimiters

a. Open the program into the Editor window.

b. Modify the program so that all occurrences of `Organization` and `Employee` are replaced with macro variable references called DSN and VAR, respectively. Submit the program and verify the output.

```
%let dsn=Organization;
%let var=Employee;
proc print data=orion.&dsn._dim;
   id &var._ID;
   var &var._Name &var._Country &var._Gender;
   title "Listing of All &var.s From Orion.&dsn._Dim";
run;
```

c. Modify the value of DSN to `Customer` and VAR to `Customer`. Resubmit the program

```
%let dsn=Customer;
%let var=Customer;
proc print data=orion.&dsn._dim;
   id &var._ID;
   var &var._Name &var._Country &var._Gender;
   title "Listing of All &var.s From Orion.&dsn._Dim";
run;
```

10. Macro Variable References with Multiple Delimiters

a. Open the program into the Editor window.

b. Using a macro variable, modify the program to return the employees with the most or least amount of seniority.

```
proc sort data=orion.staff out=staffhires;
   by Job_Title Emp_Hire_Date;
run;

%let seniority=First; /* Employees with most seniority */
/* %let seniority=Last; Employees with least seniority */

data &seniority.Hired;
   set staffhires;
   by Job_Title;
   if &seniority..Job_Title;
run;
proc print data=&seniority.Hired;
   id Job_Title;
   var Employee_ID Emp_Hire_Date;
   title "&seniority Employee Hired within Each Job Title";
run;
```

11. Using the %SUBSTR and %SCAN Functions

a. Submit a %LET statement to assign the value `Anthony Miller` to a macro variable named FULLNAME.

```
%let fullname=Anthony Miller;
```

b. Extract the first initial and last name, putting them together into a new variable as `A. Miller`.

```
%let newname=%substr(&fullname,1,1). %scan(&fullname,2);
%put &newname;
```

Alternate solution:

```
%let initial=%substr(&fullname,1,1);
%let last=%scan(&fullname,2);
%let newname=&initial.. &last;
%put &newname;
```

12. Using the %SYSFUNC Function

Use the %PUT statement and the %SYSFUNC function to display the current date and time. Format the date with the MMDDYYP10. format and the time with the TIMEAMPM. format.

```
%put Today is %sysfunc(today(), mmddyy10.) and time is
      %sysfunc(time(), timeampm.);
```

13. Using Macro Functions

a. Open the program into the Editor window.

b. The %NRSTR function is required to prevent macro variable resolution.

```
%let d=&sysdate9;
%let t=&systime;
%let product=%nrstr(R&D);
proc print data=orion.product_dim;
   where Product_Name contains "&product";
   var Product_Name Product_ID Supplier_Name;
   title1 "Product Names Containing '&product'";
   title2 "Report produced &t &d";
run;
```

14. Manipulating Macro Variables

a. Assign your birth date to a macro variable.

```
%let birthdate=06jun1982;
```

b. Issue a %PUT statement that writes the day of the week that you were born.

```
%put %sysfunc(putn("&birthdate"d,downame.));
```

Solutions to Student Activities (Polls/Quizzes)

2.01 Quiz – Correct Answers

What are the two kinds of macro variables?

Automatic and user-defined

Where are macro variables stored?

In the global symbol table

10

2.02 Quiz – Correct Answer

Submit the following statement:

```
%put _automatic_;
```

What is the value of **SYSSCPL**?

SYSSCPL is the name of the operating system being used. The value will vary. For example, the value could be XP_PRO in a Windows environment.

21

2.03 Quiz – Correct Answer

Submit program **m102d01a**.

What are the footnotes in the PROC FREQ output?

Created &systime &sysday, &sysdate9

By user &sysuserid on system &sysscpl

```
proc freq data=orion.Customer;
   table Country / nocum;
   footnote1 'Created &systime &sysday, &sysdate9';
   footnote2 'By user &sysuserid on system &sysscpl';
run;
```

35

2.04 Multiple Choice Poll – Correct Answer

Macro variable references are resolved by which
of the following?

  a. SAS compiler

  (b.) Macro processor

  c. Word scanner

49

2.05 Quiz – Correct Answer

Macro variables store numeric tokens as ...?

Text

80

2.06 Quiz – Correct Answer

How should the WHERE statement be written in the program below?

Hint: Be sure to use the CITY and SALARY macro variables.

```
%let City=New York;
%let Salary=50000;
data work.a;
   set work.b;
   where city= "&city" and salary gt &salary ;
run;
```

Use quotation marks around macro variable references when the resolved value should be enclosed in quotation marks.

91

2.07 Quiz – Correct Answer

What is the problem with this reference?

SAS interprets the macro variable's name as GRAPHICSCHART because no delimiter separates the macro variable reference from the trailing text.

Partial SAS Log

```
1    %let graphics=g;
2    %let year=2000;
3    %let month=jan;
4    %let var=sale;
5    proc &graphicschart data=orion.y&year&month;
          -
         10
WARNING: Apparent symbolic reference GRAPHICSCHART not resolved.

ERROR 10-205: Expecting the name of the procedure to be executed.
```

109

2.08 Quiz – Correct Answer

How do these references resolve?

`&lib.y&year&month` **resolves to** `oriony2000jan`.

```
libname orion 'sas-data-library';
proc gchart data=oriony2000jan;
   hbar week / sumvar=sale;
run;
proc gplot data=oriony2000jan;
   plot sale*day;
run;
```

The period after &LIB is interpreted as a delimiter, so the period does not appear as text.

115

2.09 Multiple Choice Poll – Correct Answer

What is the value of **X** after %LET statement execution?

```
%let X=%substr("ABCD",2,1);
```

(a.) A
b. B
c. C
d. D

130

2.10 Multiple Answer Poll – Correct Answers

You can use macro functions to do which of the following:

(a.) Manipulate text
(b.) Execute SAS functions
c. Manipulate SAS data set variables
(d.) Perform arithmetic

147

2.11 Quiz – Correct Answer

Submit program **m102a01**.

```
%let statement=title "Payroll Report";
%put &statement;
```

What is the value of STATEMENT?

```
title "Payroll Report"
```
Missing semicolon.

What is the potential problem with the value of STATEMENT?

The stored TITLE statement lacks a semicolon.

The semicolon ends the %LET statement.

150

Solutions to Chapter Review

Chapter Review – Correct Answers

1. Where are macro variables stored?
   In the global symbol table

2. What are the two kinds of macro variables?
   Automatic and user-defined

3. What is the maximum length of a macro variable?
   64K characters

4. How do you reference a macro variable?
   &*macro-variable-name*

158

Chapter Review – Correct Answers

5. What macro language statement creates macro variables?
   %LET

6. How can you view all user-defined macro variables?
   %PUT _user_;

7. What SAS option displays macro variable values as they are resolved?
   The SYMBOLGEN option

8. What macro language function executes SAS functions?
   %SYSFUNC

160

Chapter 3   Macro Definitions

3.1   **Defining and Calling a Macro** **3-3**

      Exercises 3-19

3.2   **Macro Parameters** **3-21**

      Exercises 3-36

3.3   **Macro Storage (Self-Study)**..**3-39**

      Exercises 3-50

3.4   **Chapter Review**...**3-52**

3.5   **Solutions** **3-53**

      Solutions to Exercises 3-53

      Solutions to Student Activities (Polls/Quizzes)...................................3-62

      Solutions to Chapter Review 3-64

3.1   Defining and Calling a Macro

Objectives

- Define and call a simple macro.

3

Defining a Macro

A *macro* or *macro definition* enables you to write macro programs.

General form of a macro definition:

```
%MACRO macro-name;
     macro-text
%MEND <macro-name>;
```

macro-name   follows SAS naming conventions.

macro-text   can include the following:

- any text
- SAS statements or steps
- macro variable references
- macro statements, expressions, or calls
- any combination of the above

4

Do not name a macro with the name of a macro statement or function (LET or SCAN, for example). Refer to the documentation for a complete list of reserved names.

Macro Compilation

When a macro definition is submitted, the following occur:

- Macro language statements, if any, are
  - checked for syntax errors
  - compiled.
- SAS statements and other text are
  - **not** checked for syntax errors
  - **not** compiled.
- The macro is stored as a SAS catalog entry in the temporary catalog **work.sasmacr** by default.

5

Macro Compilation

The MCOMPILENOTE=ALL option issues a note to the SAS log after a macro definition has compiled.

General form of the MCOMPILENOTE= option:

> **OPTIONS MCOMPILENOTE=**ALL|NONE;

The default setting is MCOMPILENOTE=NONE.

6

Macro Compilation

Example: Submit a macro definition.

```
options mcompilenote=all;
%macro time;
    %put The current time is %sysfunc
        (time(),timeampm.).;
%mend time;
```

SAS Log

```
1       options mcompilenote=all;
2       %macro time;
3           %put The current time is %sysfunc
4               (time(),timeampm.).;
5       %mend time;
NOTE: The macro TIME completed compilation without errors.
      3 instructions 76 bytes.
```

7   m103d01

Macro Storage

Example: Produce a list of compiled macros stored in the
default temporary catalog **work.sasmacr**.

```
proc catalog cat=work.sasmacr;
    contents;
    title "My Temporary Macros";
quit;
```

PROC CATALOG Output

```
                     My Temporary Macros

                Contents of Catalog WORK.SASMACR

# Name Type          Create Date          Modified Date Description
-------------------------------------------------------------------
1 TIME MACRO  11JUN2004:15:55:59   11JUN2004:15:55:59
```

m103d02

8

Calling a Macro

A *macro call*

- causes the macro to execute
- is specified by placing a percent sign before the name of the macro
- can be made anywhere in a program (similar to a macro variable reference)
- represents a macro trigger
- is **not** a statement (no semicolon required).

General form of a macro call:

```
%macro-name
```

9

Calling a Macro

Example: Call the TIME macro.

```
%time
```

SAS Log

```
178  %time
The current time is  2:49:39 PM.
```

10   m103d01

✎   Placing a semicolon after a macro call might insert an inappropriate semicolon into the resulting program, leading to errors during compilation or execution.

3.01 Poll

Does the macro call below require a semicolon?

```
%time
```

○ Yes
○ No

12

Simple Macro

A macro can generate SAS code.

Example: Write a macro that generates a PROC MEANS
step. Reference macro variables within the macro.

```
%macro calc;
   proc means data=orion.order_item &stats;
      var &vars;
   run;
%mend calc;
```

This macro contains no macro language statements.

14   m103d03

 Macro variable references within a macro definition resolve during macro execution, not compilation.

Simple Macro

Example: Call the CALC macro. Precede the call with
%LET statements that populate macro
variables referenced within the macro.

```
%let stats=min max;
%let vars=quantity;
%calc
```

15   m103d03

Program Flow

When the macro processor receives *%macro-name*,
it does the following:

1. searches the designated SAS catalog
   (**work.sasmacr** by default) for an entry named
   macro-name.MACRO

2. executes compiled macro language statements, if any

3. sends other text to the input stack for word scanning

4. pauses while the word scanner tokenizes inserted
   text, and SAS code, if any, compiles and executes

5. resumes execution of macro language statements
   after SAS code executes

16

Program Flow

Example: Submit the %LET statements and call the
          CALC macro.

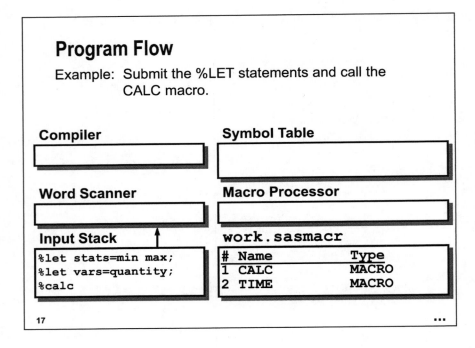

Compiler

Symbol Table

Word Scanner

Macro Processor

Input Stack

```
%let stats=min max;
%let vars=quantity;
%calc
```

work.sasmacr

#	Name	Type
1	CALC	MACRO
2	TIME	MACRO

17   ...

Program Flow

The macro processor executes the %LET statements and populates the symbol table.

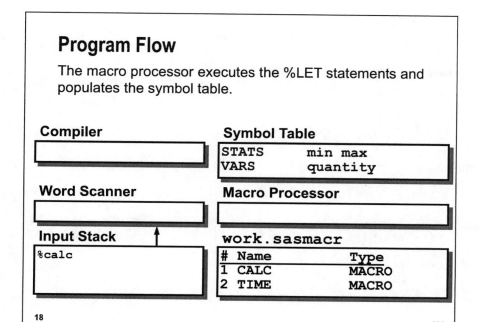

Compiler

Symbol Table

| STATS | min max |
| VARS | quantity |

Word Scanner

Macro Processor

Input Stack

`%calc`

work.sasmacr

#	Name	Type
1	CALC	MACRO
2	TIME	MACRO

18   ...

Program Flow

When the macro processor receives %CALC, it locates CALC.MACRO within the **work.sasmacr** catalog.

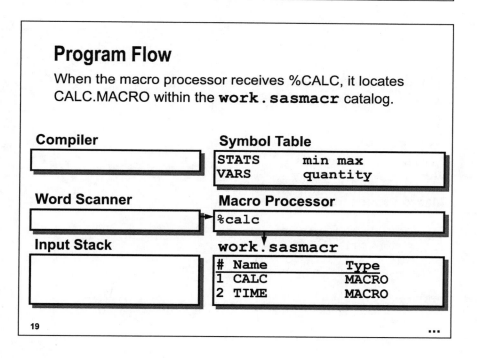

Compiler

Symbol Table

| STATS | min max |
| VARS | quantity |

Word Scanner

Macro Processor

`%calc`

Input Stack

work.sasmacr

#	Name	Type
1	CALC	MACRO
2	TIME	MACRO

19   ...

Program Flow

The macro processor opens CALC.MACRO. There are no macro language statements to execute.

Compiler

Symbol Table

STATS	min max
VARS	quantity

Word Scanner

Macro Processor

Input Stack

CALC.MACRO

```
%macro calc;
    proc means data=orion.order_item &stats;
            var &vars;
            run;
%mend calc;
```

20   •••

Program Flow

The macro processor places the macro text on the input stack.

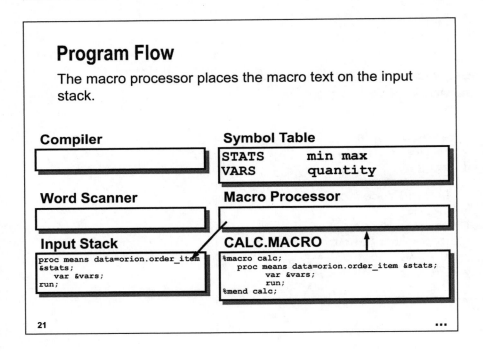

Compiler

Symbol Table

STATS	min max
VARS	quantity

Word Scanner

Macro Processor

Input Stack

```
proc means data=orion.order_item
&stats;
    var &vars;
run;
```

CALC.MACRO

```
%macro calc;
    proc means data=orion.order_item &stats;
            var &vars;
            run;
%mend calc;
```

21   •••

Program Flow

Macro activity pauses while the word scanner tokenizes text and passes it to the compiler.

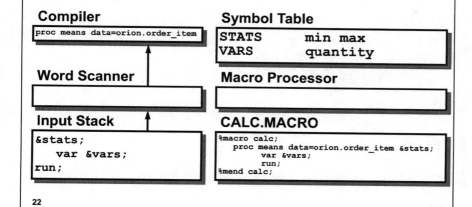

Compiler

`proc means data=orion.order_item`

Symbol Table

STATS	min max
VARS	quantity

Word Scanner

Macro Processor

Input Stack

```
&stats;
    var &vars;
run;
```

CALC.MACRO

```
%macro calc;
    proc means data=orion.order_item &stats;
        var &vars;
        run;
%mend calc;
```

22

...

Program Flow

Macro variable references are passed to the macro processor.

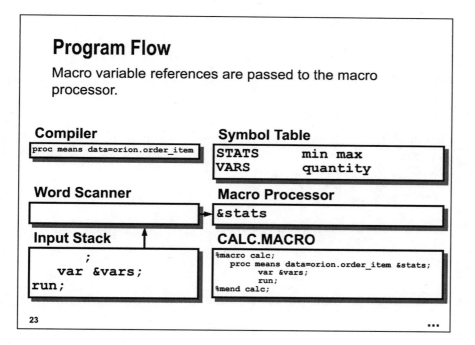

Compiler

`proc means data=orion.order_item`

Symbol Table

STATS	min max
VARS	quantity

Word Scanner

Macro Processor

`&stats`

Input Stack

```
        ;
    var &vars;
run;
```

CALC.MACRO

```
%macro calc;
    proc means data=orion.order_item &stats;
        var &vars;
        run;
%mend calc;
```

23

...

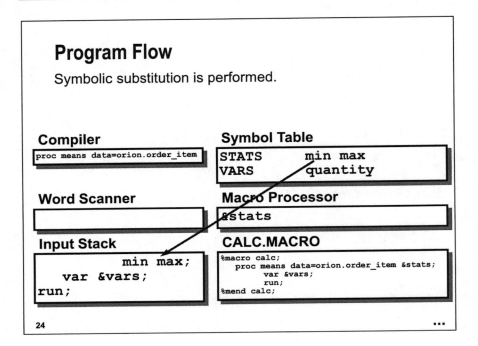

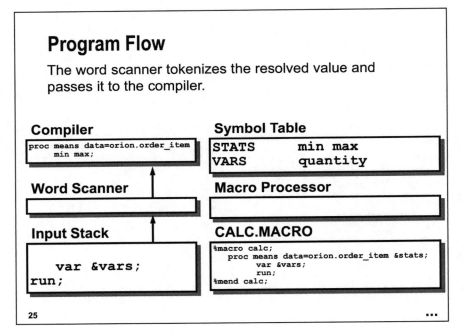

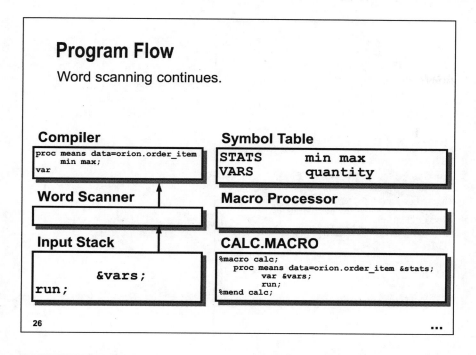

Program Flow

Word scanning continues.

Compiler
```
proc means data=orion.order_item
      min max;
var
```

Symbol Table
```
STATS        min max
VARS         quantity
```

Word Scanner

Macro Processor

Input Stack
```
            &vars;
run;
```

CALC.MACRO
```
%macro calc;
   proc means data=orion.order_item &stats;
        var &vars;
        run;
%mend calc;
```

26 ...

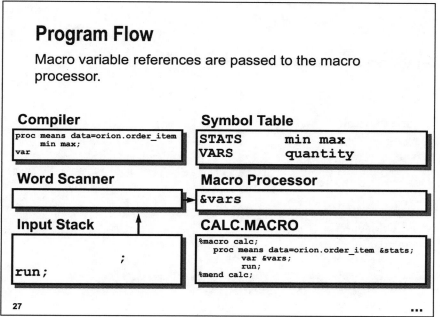

Program Flow

Macro variable references are passed to the macro processor.

Compiler
```
proc means data=orion.order_item
      min max;
var
```

Symbol Table
```
STATS        min max
VARS         quantity
```

Word Scanner

Macro Processor
```
&vars
```

Input Stack
```
            ;
run;
```

CALC.MACRO
```
%macro calc;
   proc means data=orion.order_item &stats;
        var &vars;
        run;
%mend calc;
```

27 ...

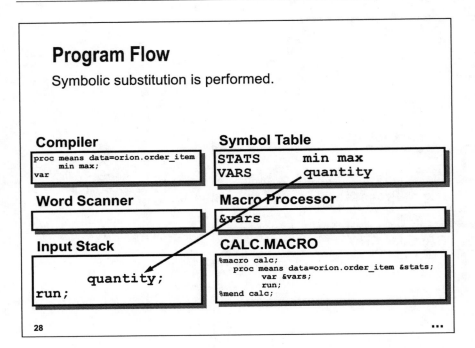

Program Flow

Symbolic substitution is performed.

Compiler

```
proc means data=orion.order_item
      min max;
var
```

Symbol Table

```
STATS        min max
VARS         quantity
```

Word Scanner

Macro Processor

```
&vars
```

Input Stack

```
          quantity;
run;
```

CALC.MACRO

```
%macro calc;
   proc means data=orion.order_item &stats;
        var &vars;
        run;
%mend calc;
```

28

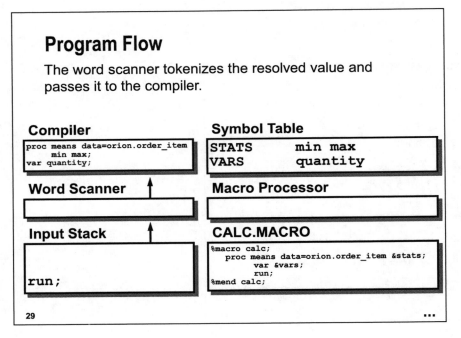

Program Flow

The word scanner tokenizes the resolved value and passes it to the compiler.

Compiler

```
proc means data=orion.order_item
      min max;
var quantity;
```

Symbol Table

```
STATS        min max
VARS         quantity
```

Word Scanner

Macro Processor

Input Stack

```
run;
```

CALC.MACRO

```
%macro calc;
   proc means data=orion.order_item &stats;
        var &vars;
        run;
%mend calc;
```

29

Program Flow

When a step boundary is encountered, SAS executes the compiled step as macro activity remains paused. Macro activity stops when the %MEND statement is encountered.

Compiler

```
proc means data=orion.order_item
         min max;
var quantity;
```

Symbol Table

```
STATS        min max
VARS         quantity
```

Word Scanner

```
run;
```

Macro Processor

Input Stack

CALC.MACRO

```
%macro calc;
   proc means data=orion.order_item &stats;
          var &vars;
          run;
%mend calc;
```

30

Macro Execution

The SAS log reflects execution of the PROC MEANS step.

SAS Log

```
52    %let stats=min max;
53    %let vars=quantity;
54    %calc

NOTE: There were 732 observations read from the data set ORION.ORDER_ITEM.
NOTE: PROCEDURE MEANS used (Total process time):
      real time           0.03 seconds
      cpu time            0.03 seconds
```

PROC MEANS source code does not appear in the SAS log.

31   m103d03

Macro Execution

The MPRINT option writes to the SAS log the text sent
to the SAS compiler as a result of macro execution.

General form of the MPRINT|NOMPRINT option:

> **OPTIONS MPRINT;**
> **OPTIONS NOMPRINT;**

The default setting is NOMPRINT.

32

Macro Execution

Example: Set the MPRINT option before calling the macro.

Partial SAS Log

```
55    options mprint;
56    %calc
MPRINT(CALC):    proc means data=orion.order_item min max;
MPRINT(CALC):    var quantity;
MPRINT(CALC):    run;

NOTE: There were 732 observations read from the data set ORION.ORDER_ITEM.
NOTE: PROCEDURE MEANS used (Total process time):
      real time            0.01 seconds
      cpu time             0.01 seconds
```

33

Macro-generated code is treated as a series of tokens. The MPRINT option writes each statement
to a new line without indention.

 **Exercises**

Level 1

1. Defining and Calling a Macro

a. Open the **m103e01** program shown below into the Editor window.

```
proc print data=orion.customer_dim;
    var Customer_Group Customer_Name Customer_Gender Customer_Age;
    where Customer_Group contains "&type";
    title "&type Customers";
run;
```

b. Convert the program into a macro named CUSTOMERS. Set the appropriate system option to display a note in the SAS log when a macro definition has compiled. Submit the macro definition and examine the log.

c. Submit a %LET statement to assign the value Gold to the macro variable TYPE. Call the macro and examine the log.

d. Change the value of TYPE to Internet.

e. Activate the appropriate system option to display source code received by the SAS compiler. Call the macro again and examine the log.

Level 2

2. Macro Storage

a. Open the **m103e02** program shown below into the Editor window.

```
%macro tut;
    king tut
%mend tut;
```

b. Submit the macro definition and check the SAS log.

c. In the SAS Explorer window, navigate to the SASMACR catalog within the Work library to locate the TUT macro.

d. Select the **TUT** macro with the right mouse button and then select **Delete**.

Level 3

3. Calling a Macro from a TITLE Statement

a. Define a macro that issues the current time of day with the TIMEAMPM. format. Name the macro CURRTIME. Submit the macro definition.

b. Open the **m103e03** program shown below into the Editor window. Add a TITLE2 statement. Call the macro from the TITLE2 statement. Submit the program and examine the output.

```
proc print data=orion.customer_dim(obs=10);
   var Customer_Name Customer_Group;
   title 'Customer List';
run;
```

3.2 Macro Parameters

Objectives

- Define and call macros with parameters.
- Describe the difference between positional parameters and keyword parameters.

37

Review

Example: Note macro variable references within the
CALC macro.

```
%macro calc;
   proc means data=orion.order_item &stats;
      var &vars;
   run;
%mend calc;
```

m103d03

38

Review

Example: Call the macro twice, each time with different
values of the macro variables STATS and
VARS.

```
%let stats=min max;
%let vars=quantity;
%calc

%let stats=n mean;
%let vars=discount;
%calc
```

The user must submit three lines each time. How can
this be simplified?

m103d03

39

Macro Parameters

Example: Define a macro with a *parameter list* of macro
variables referenced within the macro.

```
%macro calc(stats,vars);
   proc means data=orion.order_item &stats;
      var &vars;
   run;
%mend calc;
```

40   m103d05

Positional Parameters

Positional parameters use a one-to-one correspondence
between the following:

- parameter **names** supplied on the macro definition
- parameter **values** supplied on the macro call

```
%macro calc(stats,vars);
   proc means data=orion.order_item &stats;
      var &vars;
   run;
%mend calc;

%calc(min max,quantity)
```

41   m103d05

Positional Parameters

General form of a macro definition with positional parameters:

> **%MACRO** *macro-name*(*parameter-1, … parameter-n*)**;**
>   *macro text*
> **%MEND** *<macro-name>***;**

Parameter names are
- parenthesized
- comma delimited.

42

Macro Parameters

General form of a macro call with parameters:

> **%***macro-name*(*value-1, … value-n*)

Parameter values are
- parenthesized
- comma delimited.

Parameter values can be any text, null values, macro variable references, or macro calls.

43

To assign a null value to one or more positional parameters, use commas as placeholders for the omitted values.

Local Symbol Tables

When a macro with a parameter list is called, the parameters are created in a separate *local symbol table*.

The macro call

```
%calc(min max, quantity)
```

initializes a local table:

Local Table	
STATS	min max
VARS	quantity

Global Table	
SYSDAY	Tuesday
SYSLAST	_NULL_
CITY	Dallas
AMOUNT	975

44

Local Symbol Tables

A local symbol table is

- created when a macro with a parameter list is called
- deleted when the macro finishes execution.

Macro variables in the local table are available only during macro execution and can be referenced only within the macro.

45

3.02 Multiple Choice Poll

A %LET statement outside a macro definition creates
a macro variable in the

(a.) global symbol table
b. local symbol table

47

Positional Parameters

Example: Define and call a macro with positional
parameters.

```
%macro count(opts, start, stop);
   proc freq data=orion.orders;
      where order_date between
            "&start"d and "&stop"d;
      table order_type / &opts;
      title1 "Orders from &start to &stop";
   run;
%mend count;
options mprint;
%count(nocum,01jan2004,31dec2004)
%count(,01jul2004,31dec2004)
```

m103d06a

49

Macros with Positional Parameters

m103d06a

Use positional parameters to specify a range of dates and TABLE statement options for the FREQ procedure.

```
%macro count(opts, start, stop);
   proc freq data=orion.orders;
      where order_date between "&start"d and "&stop"d;
      table order_type / &opts;
      title1 "Orders from &start to &stop";
   run;
%mend count;
options mprint;
%count(nocum,01jan2004,31dec2004)
%count(,01jul2004,31dec2004)
```

   A null value is passed to the OPTS parameter in the second call.

Partial SAS Log

```
50    %count(nocum,01jan2004,31dec2004)
MPRINT(COUNT):    proc freq data=orion.orders;
MPRINT(COUNT):    where order_date between "01jan2004"d and "31dec2004"d;
MPRINT(COUNT):    table order_type / nocum;
MPRINT(COUNT):    title1 "Orders from 01jan2004 to 31dec2004";
MPRINT(COUNT):    run;
NOTE: There were 87 observations read from the data set ORION.ORDERS.
      WHERE (order_date>='01JAN2004'D and order_date<='31DEC2004'D);
NOTE: PROCEDURE FREQ used (Total process time):
      real time           0.28 seconds
      cpu time            0.11 seconds


51    %count(,01jul2004,31dec2004)
MPRINT(COUNT):    proc freq data=orion.orders;
MPRINT(COUNT):    where order_date between "01jul2004"d and "31dec2004"d;
MPRINT(COUNT):    table order_type / ;
MPRINT(COUNT):    title1 "Orders from 01jul2004 to 31dec2004";
MPRINT(COUNT):    run;
NOTE: There were 40 observations read from the data set ORION.ORDERS.
      WHERE (order_date>='01JUL2004'D and order_date<='31DEC2004'D);
NOTE: PROCEDURE FREQ used (Total process time):
      real time           0.01 seconds
      cpu time            0.01 seconds
```

Keyword Parameters

A parameter list can include keyword parameters.

General form of a macro definition with keyword parameters:

```
%MACRO macro-name(keyword=value, …, keyword=value);
    macro text
%MEND <macro-name>;
```

Keyword parameters are assigned a default value after an equal (=) sign.

51

Keyword Parameters

General form of a macro call with keyword parameters:

```
%macro-name(keyword=value, …, keyword=value)
```

keyword=value combinations can be
- specified in any order
- omitted from the call without placeholders.

If omitted from the call, a keyword parameter receives its default value.

52

To omit every keyword parameter from a macro call, specify `%macro-name()`.

Specifying `%macro-name` without the parentheses might not immediately execute the macro.

Keyword Parameters

Example: Assign default parameter values by defining
the macro with keyword parameters.

```
%macro count(opts=,start=01jan04,stop=31dec04);
   proc freq data=orion.orders;
      where order_date between
            "&start"d and "&stop"d;
      table order_type / &opts;
      title1 "Orders from &start to &stop";
   run;
%mend count;
options mprint;
%count(opts=nocum)
%count(stop=01jul04,opts=nocum nopercent)
%count()
```

m103d06b

Macros with Keyword Parameters

m103d06b

Alter the previous macro by using keyword parameters. Issue various calls to the macro.

```
%macro count(opts=,start=01jan04,stop=31dec04);
   proc freq data=orion.orders;
       where order_date between "&start"d and "&stop"d;
       table order_type / &opts;
       title1 "Orders from &start to &stop";
   run;
%mend count;
options mprint;
%count(opts=nocum)
%count(stop=01jul04,opts=nocum nopercent)
%count()
```

Partial SAS Log

```
64     %count(opts=nocum)
MPRINT(COUNT):    proc freq data=orion.orders;
MPRINT(COUNT):    where order_date between "01jan04"d and "31dec04"d;
MPRINT(COUNT):    table order_type / nocum;
MPRINT(COUNT):    title1 "Orders from 01jan04 to 31dec04";
MPRINT(COUNT):    run;
NOTE: There were 87 observations read from the data set ORION.ORDERS.
      WHERE (order_date>='01JAN2004'D and order_date<='31DEC2004'D);
NOTE: PROCEDURE FREQ used (Total process time):
      real time          0.03 seconds
      cpu time           0.03 seconds

65     %count(stop=01jul04,opts=nocum nopercent)
MPRINT(COUNT):    proc freq data=orion.orders;
MPRINT(COUNT):    where order_date between "01jan04"d and "01jul04"d;
MPRINT(COUNT):    table order_type / nocum nopercent;
MPRINT(COUNT):    title1 "Orders from 01jan04 to 01jul04";
MPRINT(COUNT):    run;
NOTE: There were 47 observations read from the data set ORION.ORDERS.
      WHERE (order_date>='01JAN2004'D and order_date<='01JUL2004'D);
NOTE: PROCEDURE FREQ used (Total process time):
      real time          0.01 seconds
      cpu time           0.01 seconds

66     %count()
MPRINT(COUNT):    proc freq data=orion.orders;
MPRINT(COUNT):    where order_date between "01jan04"d and "31dec04"d;
MPRINT(COUNT):    table order_type / ;
MPRINT(COUNT):    title1 "Orders from 01jan04 to 31dec04";
MPRINT(COUNT):    run;
NOTE: There were 87 observations read from the data set ORION.ORDERS.
      WHERE (order_date>='01JAN2004'D and order_date<='31DEC2004'D);
NOTE: PROCEDURE FREQ used (Total process time):
      real time          0.01 seconds
      cpu time           0.01 seconds
```

3.03 Quiz

Submit program **m103a01**.

```
%macro dog(name=spot);
   %put My dog is &name;
%mend dog;

%dog()
```

Edit the program to omit the parentheses.

Submit the macro call.

```
%dog
```

What do you see in the SAS log?

56

Mixed Parameter Lists

You can use a combination of positional and keyword parameters. In a *mixed parameter list*, positional parameters must be listed before keyword parameters in both the macro definition and the macro call.

58

Mixed Parameter Lists

Example: Use a combination of positional and keyword parameters.

```
%macro count(opts,start=01jan04,stop=31dec04);
   proc freq data=orion.orders;
      where order_date between
            "&start"d and "&stop"d;
      table order_type / &opts;
      title1 "Orders from &start to &stop";
   run;
%mend count;
options mprint;
%count(nocum)
%count(stop=30jun04,start=01apr04)
%count(nocum nopercent,stop=30jun04)
%count()
```

59   m103d06c

Macros with Mixed Parameter Lists

m103d06c

Alter the previous macro by using a mixed parameter list. Issue various calls to the macro.

```
%macro count(opts,start=01jan04,stop=31dec04);
proc freq data=orion.orders;
    where order_date between "&start"d and "&stop"d;
    table order_type / &opts;
    title1 "Orders from &start to &stop";
run;
%mend count;
options mprint;
%count(nocum)
%count(stop=30jun04,start=01apr04)
%count(nocum nopercent,stop=30jun04)
%count()
```

Partial SAS Log

```
76    %count(nocum)
MPRINT(COUNT):    proc freq data=orion.orders;
MPRINT(COUNT):    where order_date between "01jan04"d and "31dec04"d;
MPRINT(COUNT):    table order_type / nocum;
MPRINT(COUNT):    title1 "Orders from 01jan04 to 31dec04";
MPRINT(COUNT):    run;
NOTE: There were 87 observations read from the data set ORION.ORDERS.
      WHERE (order_date>='01JAN2004'D and order_date<='31DEC2004'D);
NOTE: PROCEDURE FREQ used (Total process time):
      real time          0.04 seconds
      cpu time           0.03 seconds


77    %count(stop=30jun04,start=01apr04)
MPRINT(COUNT):    proc freq data=orion.orders;
MPRINT(COUNT):    where order_date between "01apr04"d and "30jun04"d;
MPRINT(COUNT):    table order_type / ;
MPRINT(COUNT):    title1 "Orders from 01apr04 to 30jun04";
MPRINT(COUNT):    run;
NOTE: There were 28 observations read from the data set ORION.ORDERS.
      WHERE (order_date>='01APR2004'D and order_date<='30JUN2004'D);
NOTE: PROCEDURE FREQ used (Total process time):
      real time          0.01 seconds
      cpu time           0.01 seconds
```

(Continued on the next page.)

```
78    %count(nocum nopercent,stop=30jun04)
MPRINT(COUNT):    proc freq data=orion.orders;
MPRINT(COUNT):    where order_date between "01jan04"d and "30jun04"d;
MPRINT(COUNT):    table order_type / nocum nopercent;
MPRINT(COUNT):    title1 "Orders from 01jan04 to 30jun04";
MPRINT(COUNT):    run;
NOTE: There were 47 observations read from the data set ORION.ORDERS.
      WHERE (order_date>='01JAN2004'D and order_date<='30JUN2004'D);
NOTE: PROCEDURE FREQ used (Total process time):
      real time            0.01 seconds
      cpu time             0.01 seconds

79    %count()
MPRINT(COUNT):    proc freq data=orion.orders;
MPRINT(COUNT):    where order_date between "01jan04"d and "31dec04"d;
MPRINT(COUNT):    table order_type / ;
MPRINT(COUNT):    title1 "Orders from 01jan04 to 31dec04";
MPRINT(COUNT):    run;
NOTE: There were 87 observations read from the data set ORION.ORDERS.
      WHERE (order_date>='01JAN2004'D and order_date<='31DEC2004'D);
NOTE: PROCEDURE FREQ used (Total process time):
      real time            0.03 seconds
      cpu time             0.03 seconds
```

 **Exercises**

Level 1

4. Defining and Using Macro Parameters

a. Open the **m103e04** program shown below into the Editor window.

```
%macro customers;
proc print data=orion.customer_dim;
    var Customer_Name Customer_Gender Customer_Age;
    where Customer_Group contains "&type";
    title "&type Customers";
run;
%mend customers;
```

b. Convert this program into a macro with a positional parameter. Name the parameter based on macro variable references within the program. Set the appropriate system option to display a note in the SAS log when a macro definition has compiled. Submit the macro definition to compile the macro.

c. Call the macro defined in the previous step with a value of Gold for the parameter.

d. Call the macro again, but with a parameter value of Catalog.

e. Change the positional parameter to a keyword parameter with a default value of Club. Submit the revised macro definition to compile the macro.

f. Call the macro defined in the previous step with a value of Internet for the keyword parameter.

g. Call the macro again, but allow the macro to use its default parameter value.

Level 2

5. Using a Macro to Generate PROC MEANS Code

a. Open the **m103e05** program shown below into the Editor window.

```
options nolabel;
title 'Order Stats';
proc means data=orion.order_fact maxdec=2 mean;
   var total_retail_price;
   class order_type;
run;
title;
```

b. Create a macro with keyword parameters that generalize the code so that the following attributes are controlled by macro variables. Choose default values for all parameters so that the code executes correctly.

- Statistics: any combination of N, NMISS, MIN, MEAN, MAX, RANGE, or a null value
- Decimal places: 0, 1, 2, 3, or 4
- Analysis variables: **total_retail_price** and/or **costprice_per_unit**
- Class variables: **order_type** and/or **quantity**

c. Execute the macro using the default parameter values.

d. Call the macro again, but override all default parameter values.

e. Call the macro again, but override only the default parameter values for statistics and decimal places.

Level 3

6. Using Parameters That Contain Special Characters

a. Open the **m103e06** program shown below into the Editor window. Submit the program to compile the macro.

```
%macro specialchars(name);
   proc print data=orion.employee_addresses;
      where Employee_Name="&name";
      var Employee_ID Street_Number Street_Name City State
         Postal_Code;
      title "Data for &name";
   run;
%mend specialchars;
```

b. Execute the macro with a parameter value of Abbott, Ray.

PROC PRINT Output

			Data for Abbott, Ray			
Obs	Employee_ ID	Street_ Number	Street_Name	City	State	Postal_ Code
1	121044	2267	Edwards Mill Rd	Miami-Dade	FL	33135

3.3 Macro Storage (Self-Study)

Objectives

- Use stored compiled macros to make macros available to a SAS program.
- Use the autocall facility to make macros available to a SAS program.

64

Review

Example: Produce a list of *session-compiled* macros stored in the default temporary catalog, `work.sasmacr`.

```
proc catalog cat=work.sasmacr;
   contents;
   title "My Temporary Macros";
quit;
```

PROC CATALOG Output

```
                      My Temporary Macros

                 Contents of Catalog WORK.SASMACR

 # Name    Type      Create Date       Modified Date Description
 -------------------------------------------------------------------
 1 CALC    MACRO  15JUN2007:15:58:21   15JUN2007:15:58:21
 2 TIME    MACRO  15JUN2007:15:55:59   15JUN2007:15:55:59
```

65   m103d02

Stored Compiled Macros

The MSTORED system option enables storage of compiled macros in a permanent library.

The SASMSTORE= system option designates a permanent library to store compiled macros.

OPTIONS MSTORED **SASMSTORE=**_libref_ ;

libref   points to an allocated SAS data library.

66

Stored Compiled Macros

General form of a macro definition for permanent *stored compiled macros*:

> **%MACRO** *macro-name* / **STORE;**
>   *macro-text*
> **%MEND** *macro-name*;

The STORE option stores the compiled macro in the library indicated by the SASMSTORE= system option.

67

Stored Compiled Macros

Example: Store the CALC macro in a permanent library.

```
options mstored sasmstore=orion;
%macro calc / store;
   proc means data=orion.order_item &stats;
     var &vars;
   run;
%mend calc;
```

Call the CALC macro in a new SAS session.

```
options mstored sasmstore=orion;
%let stats=min max;
%let vars=quantity;
%calc
```

68   m103d04a

A macro stored in the **work** library takes precedence over a like-named macro in a permanent library.

Always save your macro source code.

The SASMSTORE= option can designate only a single library. To search multiple libraries, concatenate the libraries:

```
libname multi (orion,sasuser);
```

The Autocall Facility

SAS software includes an autocall library of utility macros.

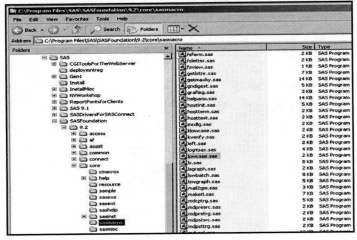

69

The Autocall Facility

An *autocall library* is a collection of external files or SAS catalog SOURCE entries that contain macro definition source code.

You can make macros accessible to your SAS session or job by concatenating your own autocall library or your organization's autocall library (or both) with the autocall library supplied with SAS software.

70

Defining an Autocall Library

To define an autocall library:

1. Specify the MAUTOSOURCE SAS system option.

2. Use the SASAUTOS= SAS system option to identify autocall library locations.

71

Autocall Facility System Options

The MAUTOSOURCE option controls autocall facility availability.

General form of the MAUTOSOURCE|NOMAUTOSOURCE option:

> **OPTIONS MAUTOSOURCE;**
> **OPTIONS NOMAUTOSOURCE;**

The default setting is MAUTOSOURCE.

72

Autocall Facility System Options

The SASAUTOS= system option specifies the location of autocall macros.

General form of the SASAUTOS= system option:

> **OPTIONS SASAUTOS=(***library-1*,...,*library-n***);**

The values of *library-1* through *library-n* are references to source libraries containing macro definitions.

You specify a source library by doing one of the following:

- placing its name in quotation marks
- pointing to it with a fileref

73

Autocall Facility System Options

Example: Concatenate the autocall library supplied by
SAS with your personal autocall library and/or
your organization's autocall library.

Windows:
```
options mautosource sasautos=('s:\workshop',sasautos);
```

UNIX:
```
options mautosource
      sasautos=('/workshop','!SASROOT/sasautos');
```

z/OS:
```
options mautosource sasautos=('my.macros',sasautos);
```

The reserved fileref SASAUTOS is assigned to the autocall library supplied by SAS.

74

The Autocall Facility in Windows or UNIX

In a Windows or UNIX environment, save each macro definition as a separate file within the directory specified in the SASAUTOS= option.

Ensure that the following are true:
- Filenames have a .sas extension.
- The filename and the macro name match.
- UNIX filenames are lowercase.

75

The Autocall Facility in z/OS

In a z/OS environment, save each macro definition as a separate member of the partitioned data set specified in the SASAUTOS= option.

The member name and the macro name must match.

A JCL DD statement with a DDname of SASAUTOS can allocate an autocall library.

76

Accessing Autocall Macros

With the autocall facility in effect, you can call any macro in the autocall library. If you call a macro that was not previously compiled, the macro facility takes these actions:

- searches the autocall library for a member with the same name as the called macro
- issues an error message if the member is not found
- executes the macro source statements to compile the macro if the member is found
- calls the macro

77

3.04 Quiz

What does the macro processor do when an autocall macro is called for the first time within a session?

79

Accessing Autocall Macros

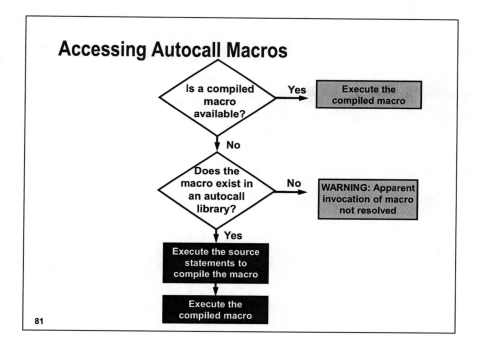

81

The Autocall Facility

Example: Save the CALC macro in an autocall library
          as `calc.sas`.

Step 1:
```
options mautosource
    sasautos=('s:\workshop',sasautos);
```

Step 2:
```
%macro calc;
   proc means data=orion.order_item &stats;
      var &vars;
   run;
%mend calc;
```

Step 3:

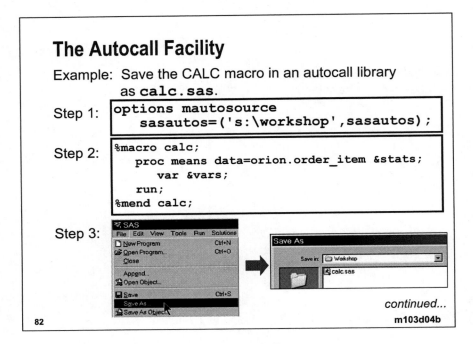

continued...

82   **m103d04b**

The Autocall Facility

Step 4: Call the CALC macro in a **new** SAS session.

```
options mautosource
        sasautos=('s:\workshop',sasautos);
%let stats=min max;
%let vars=quantity;
%calc
```

83   **m103d04b**

Macro Storage Advice

Advantages of stored compiled macros:

- You avoid re-compiling lengthy macro source code.
- Macro source code can be protected or hidden.

Advantages of autocall macros:

- They are available cross-platform.
- Macro source code can be edited in any text editor without invoking SAS.

If none of the above considerations apply, use whichever technique is preferred in your organization or whichever technique you prefer.

84

Exercises

Level 1

7. Identifying Current Autocall Settings

   a. Submit the following OPTIONS procedure step to determine whether the autocall facility is active and to determine the current location for autocall macros:

```
proc options group=macro;
run;
```

          _____

          _____

   b. If the value of the SASAUTOS= option is not a physical location, submit the following %PUT statement with the option value inserted as the fileref. The SAS log will display the physical location(s) that correspond to the fileref.

```
%put %sysfunc(pathname(fileref));
```

          🖉   The PATHNAME function returns the physical name of a SAS library or external file.

Level 2

8. Creating an Autocall Macro

   a. Add one of the following locations to your current autocall library location:

- Windows: s:\workshop
- UNIX: /local/users/*userid*
- z/OS: *userid*.WORKSHOP.SASCODE

   b. Open the **m103e08** program shown below into the Editor window. Save this macro as an autocall macro. Do not submit the macro definition.

```
%macro autocust;
   proc print data=orion.customer_dim;
      var customer_name customer_gender customer_age;
      title "Customers Listing as of &systime";
   run;
%mend autocust;
```

   c. Submit the appropriate options to activate the autocall facility and call the macro.

Level 3

9. Identifying the Location for Autocall Macros

    a. Using the Macro Language Dictionary in the SAS Help facility, identify the option to display the source code location of autocall macros.

    _____

    b. Set the above option.

    c. Add one of the following locations to your current autocall library location:
- Windows: s:\workshop
- UNIX: /local/users/*userid*
- z/OS: *userid*.WORKSHOP.SASCODE

    d. Call the CUSTOMERLIST autocall macro. What is the location of the source code?

    _____

    _____

    _____

    e. Submit the statement below and check the log.

```
%put %lowcase(FIRE);
```

    What is the location of the LOWCASE autocall macro source code? _____

    _____

    _____

3.4 Chapter Review

Chapter Review

1. What statement begins a macro definition?

2. What statement ends a macro definition?

3. What statement causes the log to display a note when a macro definition is compiled?

4. How is a macro called?

87

Chapter Review

5. What statement causes the log to display SAS code sent to the compiler as a result of macro execution?

6. What are the two types of macro parameters?

7. Where are macro parameters stored?

8. With a mixed parameter list, which type of parameter must be listed first?

89

3.5 Solutions

Solutions to Exercises

1. **Defining and Calling a Macro**

   a. Open the program into the Editor window.

   b. Convert the program into a macro named CUSTOMERS. Set the MCOMPILENOTE= option and add %MACRO and %MEND statements to create a macro definition.

   ```
   options mcompilenote=all;
   %macro customers;
      proc print data=orion.customer_dim;
         var Customer_Name Customer_Gender Customer_Age;
         where Customer_Group contains "&type";
         title "&type Customers";
      run;
   %mend customers;
   ```

   SAS Log

   ```
   1     options mcompilenote=all;
   2     %macro customers;
   3        proc print data=orion.customer_dim;
   4           var Customer_Name Customer_Gender Customer_Age;
   5           where Customer_Group contains "&type";
   6           title "&type Customers";
   7        run;
   8     %mend customers;
   NOTE: The macro CUSTOMERS completed compilation without errors.
         3 instructions 188 bytes.
   ```

   c. Submit a %LET statement to assign the value Gold to the macro variable TYPE. Call the macro by preceding its name with a percent sign.

   ```
   %let type=Gold;
   %customers
   ```

   SAS Log

   ```
   10    %let type=Gold;
   11    %customers

   NOTE: There were 21 observations read from the data set ORION.CUSTOMER_DIM.
         WHERE customer_group contains 'Gold';
   NOTE: PROCEDURE PRINT used (Total process time):
         real time           0.67 seconds
         cpu time            0.18 seconds
   ```

   d. Change the value of TYPE to Internet.

   ```
   %let type=Internet;
   ```

e. Set the appropriate system option to display source code received by the SAS compiler. Call the macro again and examine the log.

```
options mprint;
%customers
```

SAS Log

```
12    options mprint;
13    %customers
MPRINT(CUSTOMERS):    proc print data=orion.customer_dim;
MPRINT(CUSTOMERS):    var Customer_Name Customer_Gender Customer_Age;
MPRINT(CUSTOMERS):    where Customer_Group contains "Internet";
MPRINT(CUSTOMERS):    title "Internet Customers";
MPRINT(CUSTOMERS):    run;
NOTE: There were 8 observations read from the data set ORION.CUSTOMER_DIM.
      WHERE customer_group contains 'Internet';
NOTE: PROCEDURE PRINT used (Total process time):
      real time          0.01 seconds
      cpu time           0.01 seconds
```

2. **Macro Storage**

   a. Open the program into the Editor window.

   b. Submit the macro definition and check the SAS log.

   c. Use the SAS Explorer window to locate the stored macro

   d. Use the SAS Explorer window to delete the stored macro.

3. **Calling a Macro from a TITLE Statement**

   a. Define a macro that issues the current time of day with the TIMEAMPM. format. Name the macro CURRTIME. Submit the macro definition.

```
%macro currtime;
    %sysfunc(time(),timeAMPM.)
%mend currtime;
```

   b. Open the **m103e03** program into the Editor window. Add a TITLE2 statement. Call the macro from the TITLE2 statement. Submit the program and examine the output.

```
proc print data=orion.customer_dim(obs=10);
    var Customer_Name Customer_Group;
    title 'Customer List';
    title2 "%currtime";
run;
```

4. **Defining and Using Macro Parameters**

   a. Open the program into the Editor window.

   b. The macro parameter name should be TYPE because the program contains the macro references **&type**. When you define positional parameters, enclose the parameter names in parentheses following the macro name.

```
options mcompilenote=all;
```

```
%macro customers(type);
   proc print data=orion.customer_dim;
      var Customer_Name Customer_Gender Customer_Age;
      where Customer_Group contains "&type";
      title "&type Customers";
   run;
%mend customers;
```

c. To execute the macro, use a percent sign followed by the name of the macro. To assign a value to a positional parameter, supply the desired value within parentheses following the macro name.

```
options mprint;
%customers(Gold)
```

SAS Log

```
178  %customers(Gold)
MPRINT(CUSTOMERS):   proc print data=orion.customer_dim;
MPRINT(CUSTOMERS):   var Customer_Name Customer_Gender Customer_Age;
MPRINT(CUSTOMERS):   where Customer_Group contains "Gold";
MPRINT(CUSTOMERS):   title "Gold Customers";
MPRINT(CUSTOMERS):   run;
NOTE: There were 21 observations read from the data set ORION.CUSTOMER_DIM.
      WHERE customer_group contains 'Gold';
NOTE: PROCEDURE PRINT used (Total process time):
      real time           0.14 seconds
      cpu time            0.00 seconds
```

PROC PRINT Output

Gold Customers

Obs	Customer_Name	Customer_Gender	Customer_Age
2	Sandrina Stephano	F	28
3	Cornelia Krahl	F	33
7	Markus Sepke	M	19
11	Oliver S. Füßling	M	43
17	Cynthia Martinez	F	48
21	Alphone Greenwald	M	23
24	Dianne Patchin	F	28
25	Annmarie Leveille	F	23
26	Gert-Gunter Mendler	M	73
31	Carsten Maestrini	M	63
32	James Klisurich	M	38
35	Viola Folsom	F	38
40	Kyndal Hooks	F	43
46	Ramesh Trentholme	M	58
48	Avni Umran	M	28
53	Sanelisiwe Collier	F	19
57	Rita Lotz	F	43
58	Bill Cuddy	M	21
62	Susan Krasowski	F	48
64	Avinoam Tuvia	M	23
75	Angel Borwick	F	38

d. The macro definition does not need to be resubmitted with each macro call. The macro call does not end with a semicolon.

```
%customers(Catalog)
```

SAS Log

```
179  %customers(Catalog)
MPRINT(CUSTOMERS):   proc print data=orion.customer_dim;
MPRINT(CUSTOMERS):   var Customer_Name Customer_Gender Customer_Age;
MPRINT(CUSTOMERS):   where Customer_Group contains "Catalog";
MPRINT(CUSTOMERS):   title "Catalog Customers";
MPRINT(CUSTOMERS):   run;
NOTE: There were 8 observations read from the data set ORION.CUSTOMER_DIM.
      WHERE customer_group contains 'Catalog';
NOTE: PROCEDURE PRINT used (Total process time):
      real time           0.00 seconds
      cpu time            0.00 seconds
```

PROC PRINT Output

```
                       Catalog Customers

                       Customer_     Customer_
    Obs    Customer_Name   Gender        Age

     8     Ulrich Heyde       M           68
    13     Tulio Devereaux    M           58
    14     Robyn Klem         F           48
    15     Cynthia Mccluney   F           38
    16     Candy Kinsey       F           73
    20     Phenix Hill        M           43
    59     Avinoam Zweig      M           48
    67     Lauren Marx        F           38
```

e. When you define keyword parameters, an equal sign (=) must follow the name of each parameter. A default value for each parameter can be specified following the equal sign.

```
%macro customers(type=Club);
   proc print data=orion.customer_dim;
      var Customer_Name Customer_Gender Customer_Age;
      where Customer_Group contains "&type";
      title "&type Customers";
   run;
%mend customers;
```

f. To assign a value to a keyword parameter, specify the name of the parameter followed by an equal sign (=), followed by the desired value.

```
%customers(type=Internet)
```

SAS Log

```
180    %customers(type=Internet)
MPRINT(CUSTOMERS):    proc print data=orion.customer_dim;
MPRINT(CUSTOMERS):    var Customer_Name Customer_Gender Customer_Age;
MPRINT(CUSTOMERS):    where Customer_Group contains "Internet";
MPRINT(CUSTOMERS):    title "Internet Customers";
MPRINT(CUSTOMERS):    run;
NOTE: There were 8 observations read from the data set ORION.CUSTOMER_DIM.
      WHERE customer_group contains 'Internet';
NOTE: PROCEDURE PRINT used (Total process time):
      real time            0.00 seconds
      cpu time             0.00 seconds
```

PROC PRINT Output

```
                  Internet Customers

                       Customer_     Customer_
Obs    Customer_Name    Gender         Age

  8    Ulrich Heyde        M            68
 13    Tulio Devereaux     M            58
 14    Robyn Klem          F            48
 15    Cynthia Mccluney    F            38
 16    Candy Kinsey        F            73
 20    Phenix Hill         M            43
 59    Avinoam Zweig       M            48
 67    Lauren Marx         F            38
```

g. To request that all default parameter values be used, follow the macro call with empty parentheses.

```
%customers()
```

SAS Log

```
189  %customers()
MPRINT(CUSTOMERS):    proc print data=orion.customer_dim;
MPRINT(CUSTOMERS):    var Customer_Name Customer_Gender Customer_Age;
MPRINT(CUSTOMERS):    where Customer_Group contains "Club";
MPRINT(CUSTOMERS):    title "Club Customers";
MPRINT(CUSTOMERS):    run;
NOTE: There were 69 observations read from the data set ORION.CUSTOMER_DIM.
      WHERE customer_group contains 'Club';
NOTE: PROCEDURE PRINT used (Total process time):
      real time            0.00 seconds
      cpu time             0.00 seconds
```

5. **Using a Macro to Generate PROC MEANS Code**

a. Open the program into the Editor window.

b. Create a macro with keyword parameters that generalize the code so that the following attributes are controlled by macro variables. Choose default values for all parameters so that the code executes correctly.

```
%macro orderstats
   (var=total_retail_price,class=order_type,stats=mean,decimals=2);
      options nolabel;
      title 'Order Stats';
      proc means data=orion.order_fact maxdec=&decimals &stats;
         var &var;
         class &class;
      run;
      title;
%mend orderstats;
```

c. Execute the macro using the default parameter values.

```
%orderstats()
```

SAS Log

```
85   %orderstats()
MPRINT(ORDERSTATS):   options nolabel;
MPRINT(ORDERSTATS):   title 'Order Stats';
MPRINT(ORDERSTATS):   proc means data=orion.order_fact maxdec=2 mean;
MPRINT(ORDERSTATS):   var total_retail_price;
MPRINT(ORDERSTATS):   class order_type;
MPRINT(ORDERSTATS):   run;

NOTE: Multiple concurrent threads will be used to summarize data.
NOTE: There were 617 observations read from the data set ORION.ORDER_FACT.
NOTE: PROCEDURE MEANS used (Total process time):
      real time            0.04 seconds
      cpu time             0.04 seconds

MPRINT(ORDERSTATS):   title;
```

d. Call the macro again, but override all default parameter values.

```
%orderstats(var=costprice_per_unit, class=quantity, stats=min mean max, decimals=0)
```

SAS Log

```
 86    %orderstats(var=costprice_per_unit, class=quantity, stats=min mean max, decimals=0)
MPRINT(ORDERSTATS):    options nolabel;
MPRINT(ORDERSTATS):    title 'Order Stats';
MPRINT(ORDERSTATS):    proc means data=orion.order_fact maxdec=0 min mean max;
MPRINT(ORDERSTATS):    var costprice_per_unit;
MPRINT(ORDERSTATS):    class quantity;
MPRINT(ORDERSTATS):    run;

NOTE: Multiple concurrent threads will be used to summarize data.
NOTE: There were 617 observations read from the data set ORION.ORDER_FACT.
NOTE: PROCEDURE MEANS used (Total process time):
      real time            0.04 seconds
      cpu time             0.04 seconds

MPRINT(ORDERSTATS):    title;
```

e. Call the macro again, but override only the default parameter values for statistics and decimal places.

```
%orderstats(stats=min mean max, decimals=0)
```

SAS Log

```
 87    %orderstats(stats=min mean max, decimals=0)
MPRINT(ORDERSTATS):    options nolabel;
MPRINT(ORDERSTATS):    title 'Order Stats';
MPRINT(ORDERSTATS):    proc means data=orion.order_fact maxdec=0 min mean max;
MPRINT(ORDERSTATS):    var total_retail_price;
MPRINT(ORDERSTATS):    class order_type;
MPRINT(ORDERSTATS):    run;

NOTE: Multiple concurrent threads will be used to summarize data.
NOTE: There were 617 observations read from the data set ORION.ORDER_FACT.
NOTE: PROCEDURE MEANS used (Total process time):
      real time            0.04 seconds
      cpu time             0.04 seconds

MPRINT(ORDERSTATS):    title;
```

6. **Using Parameters That Contain Special Characters**

   a. Open the program into the Editor window. Submit the program to compile the macro.

   b. The %STR function is required to prevent a special character such as a comma from being misinterpreted as a parameter delimiter on the macro call.

   ```
   options mprint;
   %specialchars(%str(Abbott, Ray))
   ```

   SAS Log

   ```
   63   %specialchars(%str(Abbott, Ray))
   MPRINT(SPECIALCHARS):   proc print data=orion.employee_addresses;
   MPRINT(SPECIALCHARS):   where Employee_Name="Abbott, Ray";
   MPRINT(SPECIALCHARS):   var Employee_ID Street_Number Street_Name City State Postal_Code;
   MPRINT(SPECIALCHARS):   title "Data for Abbott, Ray";
   MPRINT(SPECIALCHARS):   run;
   NOTE: There were 1 observations read from the data set ORION.EMPLOYEE_ADDRESSES.
         WHERE Employee_Name='Abbott, Ray';
   NOTE: PROCEDURE PRINT used (Total process time):
         real time           2.51 seconds
         cpu time            0.00 seconds
   ```

7. **Identifying Current Autocall Settings**

   a. By default, the autocall facility is available through the MAUTOSOURCE option. The value for the SASAUTOS= system option is SASAUTOS.

   b. The PATHNAME function returns the physical name of a SAS library or external file.

   ```
   %put %sysfunc(pathname(sasautos));
   ```

8. **Creating an Autocall Macro**

   a. Add one of the following locations to your current autocall library location.

   ```
   options sasautos=('s:\workshop', sasautos);     /* Windows */
   /* options sasautos=('.','!SASROOT/sasautos');           UNIX */
   /* options sasautos=('.workshop.sascode', sasautos); z/OS */
   ```

   b. Save your SAS program to a file named **autocust.sas** by selecting **File** ⇨ **Save As....**

   c. Submit the MAUTOSOURCE option to activate the autocall facility and call the macro.

   ```
   options mautosource;
   %autocust
   ```

9. Identifying the Location for Autocall Macros

a. The MAUTOLOCDISPLAY option displays the location of the source code for autocall macros in the SAS log. The default setting for this option is NOMAUTOLOCDISPLAY.

b. Set the above option.

```
options mautolocdisplay;
```

c. Add one of the following locations to your current autocall library location.

```
options sasautos=('s:\workshop', sasautos);       /* Windows */
/* options sasautos=('.','!SASROOT/sasautos');          UNIX */
/* options sasautos=('.workshop.sascode', sasautos); z/OS */
```

d. Call the CUSTOMERLIST autocall macro.

```
%customerlist
```

The location of the source code is as follows:

- Windows: s:\workshop
- UNIX: /users
- z/OS: *userid*.workshop.sascode

e. The location of the LOWCASE autocall macro is as follows:

- Windows: C:\Program Files\SAS\SAS 9.2\core\sasmacro\lowcase.sas
- UNIX: /local/sas92/sasautos/lowcase.sas
- z/OS: SDC.SAS9CURR.W0.AUTOLIB(LOWCASE)

   The location of SAS autocall macros is site-dependant and might differ from the above.

Solutions to Student Activities (Polls/Quizzes)

3.01 Poll – Correct Answer

Does the macro call below require a semicolon?

```
%time
```

○ Yes

◉ No

A macro call is not a statement. A semicolon is not required and can cause problems.

13

3.02 Multiple Choice Poll – Correct Answer

A %LET statement outside a macro definition creates a macro variable in the

(a.) global symbol table
 b. local symbol table

48

3.03 Quiz – Correct Answer

Edit the program to omit the parentheses.
Submit the macro call.

```
%dog
```

What do you see in the SAS log?

```
67    %dog()
My dog is spot
68    %dog
```

The macro call will not execute without parentheses.

57

3.04 Quiz – Correct Answer

What does the macro processor do when an autocall
macro is called for the first time within a session?

**The macro processor compiles an autocall macro the
first time the macro is called within the session.**

80

Solutions to Chapter Review

Chapter Review – Correct Answers

1. What statement begins a macro definition?
   %MACRO

2. What statement ends a macro definition?
   %MEND

3. What statement causes the log to display a note when a macro definition is compiled?
   OPTIONS MCOMPILENOTE=ALL;

4. How is a macro called?
   %macro-name

88

Chapter Review – Correct Answers

5. What statement causes the log to display SAS code sent to the compiler as a result of macro execution?
   OPTIONS MPRINT;

6. What are the two types of macro parameters?
   Positional parameters and keyword parameters

7. Where are macro parameters stored?
   In a local symbol table

8. With a mixed parameter list, which type of parameter must be listed first?
   Positional parameters

90

Chapter 4   DATA Step and SQL Interfaces

4.1   **Creating Macro Variables in the DATA Step** **4-3**

     Exercises 4-23

4.2   **Indirect References to Macro Variables** **4-26**

     Demonstration: Indirect References to Macro Variables (Self-Study) 4-39

     Exercises 4-40

4.3   **Retrieving Macro Variables in the DATA Step (Self-Study)** **4-43**

     Exercises 4-47

4.4   **Creating Macro Variables in SQL** **4-49**

     Exercises 4-58

4.5   **Chapter Review** **4-62**

4.6   **Solutions** **4-63**

     Solutions to Exercises 4-63

     Solutions to Student Activities (Polls/Quizzes) 4-72

     Solutions to Chapter Review 4-75

4.1 Creating Macro Variables in the DATA Step

Objectives

- Create macro variables during DATA step execution.
- Describe the difference between the SYMPUTX routine and the %LET statement.

3

The DATA Step Interface

Example: Automate production of the report below,
          with an appropriate footnote. Internet orders
          have an **Order_Type** of 3.

```
                         Orders for 2-2007

              Order_      Order_                    Total_Retail_
     Obs       Date        Type     Quantity           Price

      1      05FEB2007       1          1              $117.60
      2      07FEB2007       1          2              $656.60
      3      07FEB2007       1          2              $129.00
      4      09FEB2007       1          2               $36.20
      5      16FEB2007       1          1               $29.40
      6      28FEB2007       1          5              $192.00



                       No Internet Orders
```

4

Many applications require macro variables to store values based on data, programming logic, or expressions.

The DATA Step Interface

```
%let month=2;
%let year=2007;

data orders;
   keep order_date order_type quantity total_retail_price;
   set orion.order_fact end=final;
   where year(order_date)=&year and month(order_date)=&month;
   if order_type=3 then Number+1;
   if final then do;
      put Number=;
      if Number=0 then do;
         %let foot=No Internet Orders;
      end;
      else do;
         %let foot=Some Internet Orders;
      end;
   end;
run;

proc print data=orders;
   title "Orders for &month-&year";
   footnote "&foot";
run;
```

5   m104d01a

The DATA Step Interface

Why is the footnote incorrect?

```
                      Orders for 2-2007

             Order_    Order_                    Total_Retail_
   Obs       Date      Type      Quantity        Price

    1       05FEB2007    1           1             $117.60
    2       07FEB2007    1           2             $656.60
    3       07FEB2007    1           2             $129.00
    4       09FEB2007    1           2              $36.20
    5       16FEB2007    1           1              $29.40
    6       28FEB2007    1           5             $192.00




                      Some Internet Orders
```

6

The DATA Step Interface

Word scanning begins. Macro triggers are encountered.

```
%let month=2;
%let year=2007;
data orders;
   keep order_date order_type quantity total_retail_price;
   set orion.order_fact end=final;
   where year(order_date)=&year and month(order_date)=&month;
   if order_type=3 then Number+1;
   if final then do;
      put Number=;
      if Number=0 then do;
         %let foot=No Internet Orders;
         end;
      else do;
         %let foot=Some Internet Orders;
         end;
      end;
run;
```

Symbol Table

month	2
year	2007

7

...

The DATA Step Interface

Compiling begins. Macro variable references are resolved.

```
data orders;
   keep order_date order_type quantity total_retail_price;
   set orion.order_fact end=final;
   where year(order_date)=2007 and month(order_date)=2;
   if order_type=3 then Number+1;
   if final then do;
      put Number=;
      if Number=0 then do;
         %let foot=No Internet Orders;
         end;
      else do;
         %let foot=Some Internet Orders;
         end;
      end;
run;
```

Symbol Table

month	2
year	2007

8   ...

The DATA Step Interface

The macro trigger is passed to the macro processor.

```
data orders;
   keep order_date order_type quantity total_retail_price;
   set orion.order_fact end=final;
   where year(order_date)=2007 and month(order_date)=2;
   if order_type=3 then Number+1;
   if final then do;
      put Number=;
      if Number=0 then do;
         %let foot=No Internet Orders;
         end;
      else do;
         %let foot=Some Internet Orders;
         end;
      end;
run;
```

Symbol Table

month	2
year	2007
foot	No Internet Orders

9   ...

The DATA Step Interface

The macro variable FOOT is assigned.

```
data orders;
   keep order_date order_type quantity total_retail_price;
   set orion.order_fact end=final;
   where year(order_date)=2007 and month(order_date)=2;
   if order_type=3 then Number+1;
   if final then do;
      put Number=;
      if Number=0 then do;

         end;
      else do;
         %let foot=Some Internet Orders;
         end;
      end;
run;
```

Symbol Table

month	2
year	2007
foot	No Internet Orders

10   •••

The DATA Step Interface

The macro trigger overwrites the previous value.

```
data orders;
   keep order_date order_type quantity total_retail_price;
   set orion.order_fact end=final;
   where year(order_date)=2007 and month(order_date)=2;
   if order_type=3 then Number+1;
   if final then do;
      put Number=;
      if Number=0 then do;

         end;
      else do;
         %let foot=Some Internet Orders;
         end;
      end;
run;
```

Symbol Table

month	2
year	2007
foot	Some Internet Orders

11   •••

%LET statements execute at word-scanning time. SAS statements are sent to the compiler.

The DATA Step Interface

The compile phase is complete. Ready for execution.

```
data orders;
   keep order_date order_type quantity total_retail_price;
   set orion.order_fact end=final;
   where year(order_date)=2007 and month(order_date)=2;
   if order_type=3 then Number+1;
   if final then do;
      put Number=;
      if Number=0 then do;

         end;
      else do;

         end;
      end;
run;
```

Symbol Table

month	2
year	2007
foot	Some Internet Orders

Nothing in this DATA step affects the value of FOOT.

It remains
`Some Internet Orders.`

12

The SYMPUTX Routine

The SYMPUTX routine assigns to a macro variable any value available to the DATA step during execution time.

It can create macro variables with the following:

- static values
- dynamic (data dependent) values
- dynamic (data dependent) names

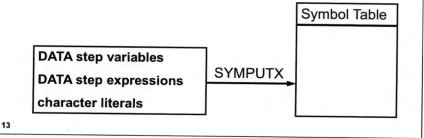

13

The SYMPUTX routine was introduced in SAS®9. In prior versions of SAS, the SYMPUT routine was available.

The SYMPUTX Routine

The SYMPUTX routine is an **executable** DATA step statement.

General form of the CALL SYMPUTX statement:

> **CALL SYMPUTX(***macro-variable, text***);**

macro-variable is assigned the character value of *text*.

If *macro-variable* already exists, its value is replaced.

Literal values in either argument must be enclosed in quotation marks.

14

The SYMPUTX Routine

Example: The SYMPUTX routine can be controlled with
DATA step execution-time logic.

No macro triggers within DO groups

```
%let month=2;
%let year=2007;

data orders;
   keep order_date order_type quantity total_retail_price;
   set orion.order_fact end=final;
   where year(order_date)=&year and month(order_date)=&month;
   if order_type=3 then Number+1;
   if final then do;
      put Number=;
      if Number=0 then do;
         call symputx('foot', 'No Internet Orders');
      end;
      else do;
         call symputx('foot', 'Some Internet Orders');
      end;
   end;
run;
```

Fixed macro variable name

Fixed macro variable value

m104d01b

15

Macro variables created by the SYMPUTX routine are available following DATA step execution and can be referenced after a step boundary.

The SYMPUTX Routine

The footnote is correct.

```
                      Orders for 2-2007

                 Order_    Order_              Total_Retail_
        Obs       Date      Type    Quantity      Price

         1      05FEB2007     1         1         $117.60
         2      07FEB2007     1         2         $656.60
         3      07FEB2007     1         2         $129.00
         4      09FEB2007     1         2          $36.20
         5      16FEB2007     1         1          $29.40
         6      28FEB2007     1         5         $192.00



                        No Internet Orders
```

16

The SYMPUTX Routine

m104d01b

Conditionally assign a text value to a macro variable FOOT based on DATA step values. Reference this macro variable later in the program.

```
%let month=2;
%let year=2007;

data orders;
   keep order_date order_type quantity total_retail_price;
   set orion.order_fact end=final;
   where year(order_date)=&year and month(order_date)=&month;
   if order_type=3 then Number+1;
   if final then do;
      put Number=;
      if Number=0 then do;
         call symputx('foot', 'No Internet Orders');
      end;
      else do;
         call symputx('foot', 'Some Internet Orders');
      end;
   end;
run;

proc print data=orders;
   title "Orders for &month-&year";
   footnote "&foot";
run;
```

The value assigned to the macro variable FOOT is set dynamically to No Internet Orders or Some Internet Orders, based on DATA step execution-time logic.

PROC PRINT Output

```
                     Orders for 2-2007

            Order_    Order_                  Total_Retail_
   Obs       Date      Type     Quantity         Price

    1      05FEB2007     1          1           $117.60
    2      07FEB2007     1          2           $656.60
    3      07FEB2007     1          2           $129.00
    4      09FEB2007     1          2            $36.20
    5      16FEB2007     1          1            $29.40
    6      28FEB2007     1          5           $192.00



            No Internet Orders
```

4.01 Multiple Choice Poll

What is the value of FOOT after execution of the DATA step?

```
data _null_;
   call symputx('foot','No internet orders');
   %let foot=Some internet orders;
run;
```

a. No internet orders

b. Some internet orders

19

The SYMPUTX Routine

Example: Enhance the footnote.

```
                        Orders for 1-2007

              Order_    Order_                   Total_Retail_
       Obs     Date      Type     Quantity           Price

        1    02JAN2007     3          2             $195.60
        2    03JAN2007     1          6             $160.80
        3    04JAN2007     1          2             $306.20
        4    06JAN2007     3          3              $37.80
        5    13JAN2007     1          2             $362.60
        6    23JAN2007     1          1              $72.60
        7    24JAN2007     1          2             $258.20
        8    24JAN2007     1          2              $81.20
        9    24JAN2007     1          3             $358.20
       10    25JAN2007     3          1             $102.40
       11    25JAN2007     3          1             $113.20
       12    28JAN2007     3          2             $174.40
       13    29JAN2007     2          1              $37.40

                        5 Internet Orders
```

21

The SYMPUTX Routine

You can copy the current value of a DATA step variable into a macro variable by using the name of a DATA step variable as the second argument to the SYMPUTX routine.

CALL SYMPUTX('*macro-variable*', *DATA-step-variable*);

- A maximum of 32,767 characters can be assigned to the receiving macro variable.
- Values of numeric variables are automatically converted to character using the BEST. format, with a field width up to 32 characters.
- Leading and trailing blanks are automatically removed from both arguments.

22

The SYMPUT routine, which remains available, has syntax and functionality that is similar to that of the SYMPUTX routine. The SYMPUT routine does not automatically trim leading and trailing blanks from either argument. Therefore, it is often necessary to use TRIM and LEFT functions within the SYMPUT routine. When assigning numeric values to macro variables, the SYMPUT routine writes numeric-to-character conversion notes to the log.

The SYMPUTX Routine

```
%let month=1;
%let year=2007;

data orders;
   keep order_date order_type quantity total_retail_price;
   set orion.order_fact end=final;
   where year(order_date)=&year and month(order_date)=&month;
   if order_type=3 then Number+1;
   if final then call symputx('num', Number);
run;

proc print data=orders;
   title "Orders for &month-&year";
   footnote "&num Internet Orders";
run;
```

m104d01c

23

The SYMPUTX Routine

m104d01c

```
%let month=1;
%let year=2007;

data orders;
   keep order_date order_type quantity total_retail_price;
   set orion.order_fact end=final;
   where year(order_date)=&year and month(order_date)=&month;
   if order_type=3 then Number+1;
   if final then call symputx('num', Number);
run;

proc print data=orders;
   title "Orders for &month-&year";
   footnote "&num Internet Orders";
run;
```

PROC PRINT Output

```
                      Orders for 1-2007

                 Order_     Order_                Total_Retail_
          Obs      Date       Type    Quantity       Price

           1     02JAN2007      3          2         $195.60
           2     03JAN2007      1          6         $160.80
           3     04JAN2007      1          2         $306.20
           4     06JAN2007      3          3          $37.80
           5     13JAN2007      1          2         $362.60
           6     23JAN2007      1          1          $72.60
           7     24JAN2007      1          2         $258.20
           8     24JAN2007      1          2          $81.20
           9     24JAN2007      1          3         $358.20
          10     25JAN2007      3          1         $102.40
          11     25JAN2007      3          1         $113.20
          12     28JAN2007      3          2         $174.40
          13     29JAN2007      2          1          $37.40

                      5 Internet Orders
```

The SYMPUTX Routine

Example: Further enhance the footnotes.

```
                    Orders for 1-2007

              Order_    Order_                  Total_Retail_
      Obs      Date      Type     Quantity         Price

       1     02JAN2007     3         2            $195.60
       2     03JAN2007     1         6            $160.80
       3     04JAN2007     1         2            $306.20
       4     06JAN2007     3         3             $37.80
       5     13JAN2007     1         2            $362.60
       6     23JAN2007     1         1             $72.60
       7     24JAN2007     1         2            $258.20
       8     24JAN2007     1         2             $81.20
       9     24JAN2007     1         3            $358.20
      10     25JAN2007     3         1            $102.40
      11     25JAN2007     3         1            $113.20
      12     28JAN2007     3         2            $174.40
      13     29JAN2007     2         1             $37.40

               Average Internet Order: $125
               Last Internet Order: 01/28/2007
```

25

The data set is sorted by `Order_Date`.

The SYMPUTX Routine

You can use DATA step functions and expressions in the SYMPUTX routine's second argument to do the following:

- format data values
- perform arithmetic operations on numeric data
- manipulate character data

> **CALL SYMPUTX**('*macro-variable*',*expression*);

26

The SYMPUTX Routine

m104d01d

```
%let month=1;
%let year=2007;
data orders;
   keep order_date order_type quantity total_retail_price;
   set orion.order_fact end=final;
   where year(order_date)=&year and month(order_date)=&month;
   if order_type=3 then do;
      Number+1;
      Amount+total_retail_price;
      Date=order_date;
      retain date;
      end;
   if final then do;
      if number=0 then do;
         call symputx('dat', 'N/A');
         call symputx('avg', 'N/A');
         end;
      else do;
         call symputx('dat', put(date,mmddyy10.));
         call symputx('avg', put(amount/number,dollar8.));
         end;
      end;
run;
proc print data=orders;
   title "Orders for &month-&year";
   footnote1 "Average Internet Order: &avg";
   footnote2 "Last Internet Order: &dat";
run;
```

The PUT function returns a character string by writing a value with a specified format.

You can use the PUT function to do the following:

- format the result of a numeric expression
- perform explicit numeric-to-character conversion

General form of the PUT function:

> **PUT**(*source*, *format*)

source is a constant, variable, or expression (numeric or character).

format is any SAS format or user-defined format. It determines the width of the resulting string and whether the string is right-aligned or left-aligned. The type for *format* must match the type for *source*.

PROC PRINT Output

```
                    Orders for 1-2007

             Order_      Order_                    Total_Retail_
    Obs       Date        Type       Quantity         Price

     1      02JAN2007       3           2            $195.60
     2      03JAN2007       1           6            $160.80
     3      04JAN2007       1           2            $306.20
     4      06JAN2007       3           3             $37.80
     5      13JAN2007       1           2            $362.60
     6      23JAN2007       1           1             $72.60
     7      24JAN2007       1           2            $258.20
     8      24JAN2007       1           2             $81.20
     9      24JAN2007       1           3            $358.20
    10      25JAN2007       3           1            $102.40
    11      25JAN2007       3           1            $113.20
    12      28JAN2007       3           2            $174.40
    13      29JAN2007       2           1             $37.40

               Average Internet Order: $125
              Last Internet Order: 01/28/2007
```

4.02 Quiz

Open program **m104a01**.

Edit the CALL SYMPUTX routines to format values.
- Display DAT as a date such as 11/21/2009.
- Display AVG as a number with dollar signs and no decimal places.

```
call symputx('dat', put(date,          ));
call symputx('avg', put(amount/number, ));
```

Submit the edited program.

29

Passing Values between Steps

Example: Based on user-selected time periods, dynamically compute statistics for automatic inclusion within titles, footnotes, and a graphic reference line.

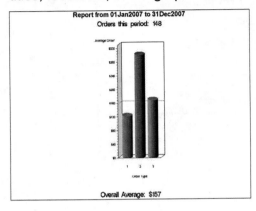

32

Passing Values between Steps

```
%let start=01Jan2007;
%let stop=31Dec2007;
proc means data=orion.order_fact noprint;
    where order_date between "&start"d and "&stop"d;
    var total_retail_price;
    output out=stats n=count mean=avg;
run;
data _null_;
    set stats;
    call symputx('orders',count);
    call symputx('average',avg);
run;
proc gchart data=orion.order_fact;
    where order_date between "&start"d and "&stop"d;
    vbar3d order_type
        / patternid=midpoint shape=c discrete raxis=0 to 320 by 40
          sumvar=total_retail_price type=mean ref=&average;
    format total_retail_price dollar4.;
    label total_retail_price='Average Order';
    title1 h=1 "Report from &start to &stop";
    title2 h=1 f=swiss "Orders this period: " c=b "&orders";
    footnote1 h=1 f=swiss "Overall Average: " c=b
        "%sysfunc(putn(&average,dollar4.))";
run;
```

Same data set

m104d02

✎   The PUTN function returns a character string by writing a value with a numeric format.

✎   PROC GCHART requires SAS/GRAPH software.

Passing Values between Steps

m104d02

```
%let start=01Jan2007;
%let stop=31Dec2007;

proc means data=orion.order_fact noprint;
   where order_date between "&start"d and "&stop"d;
   var total_retail_price;
   output out=stats n=count mean=avg;
   run;

data _null_;
   set stats;
   call symputx('orders',count);
   call symputx('average',avg);
run;

proc gchart data=orion.order_fact;
   where order_date between "&start"d and "&stop"d;
   vbar3d order_type
      / patternid=midpoint shape=c discrete raxis=0 to 320 by 40
        sumvar=total_retail_price type=mean ref=&average;
   format total_retail_price dollar4.;
   label total_retail_price='Average Order';
   title1 h=1 "Report from &start to &stop";
   title2 h=1 f=swiss "Orders this period: " c=b "&orders";
   footnote1 h=1 f=swiss "Overall Average: " c=b
      "%sysfunc(putn(&average,dollar4.))";
run;
quit;
```

PROC GCHART Output

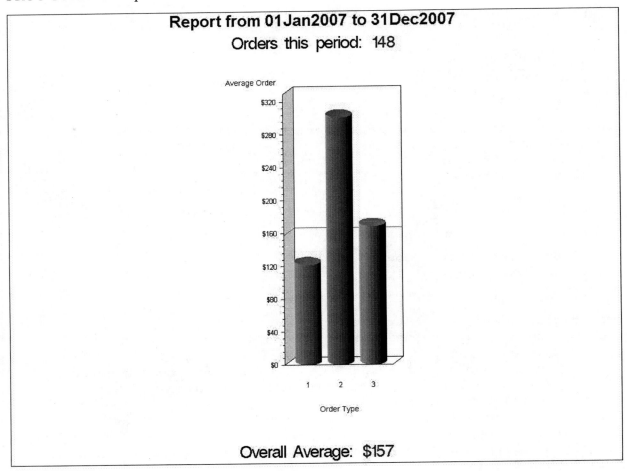

PROC CHART is a Base SAS alternative to PROC GCHART.

```
proc chart data=orion.order_fact;
   where order_date between "&start"d and "&stop"d;
   vbar order_type / discrete axis=0 to 320 by 40
        sumvar=total_retail_price type=mean ref=&average;
   format total_retail_price dollar4.;
   label total_retail_price='Average Order';
   title1 "Report from &start to &stop";
   title2 "Orders this period: " "&orders";
   footnote1 "Overall Average: %sysfunc(putn(&average,dollar4.))";
run;
```

 **Exercises**

Level 1

1. **Creating Macro Variables with the SYMPUTX Routine**

   a. Open the **m104e01** program shown below into the Editor window. Submit the program and examine the output that it creates.

   ```
   %macro emporders(idnum=121044);
      proc print data=orion.orders noobs;
         var Order_ID Order_Type Order_Date Delivery_Date;
         where Employee_ID=&idnum;
         title "Orders Taken by Employee &idnum";
      run;
   %mend emporders;

   %emporders()
   ```

   b. Modify the macro to include a DATA step that creates a macro variable named NAME based on the variable **Employee_Name** found in the **orion.employee_addresses** data set.

   c. Modify the TITLE statement to display the name of the employee instead of the employee's ID number. Call the macro using the default parameter value.

   PROC PRINT Output

   ```
                        Orders Taken by Employee  Abbott, Ray

                        Order_        Order_      Delivery_
            Order_ID     Type          Date          Date

           1231468750      1         25SEP2003     30SEP2003
           1238367238      1         31JAN2006     31JAN2006
           1238686430      1         12MAR2006     12MAR2006
           1240903120      1         14DEC2006     14DEC2006
   ```

   d. Call the macro again, but with a parameter value of `121066`.

   PROC PRINT Output

   ```
                        Orders Taken by Employee Norman, Ceresh

                        Order_        Order_      Delivery_
            Order_ID     Type          Date          Date

           1230498538      1         01APR2003     01APR2003
           1232007700      1         31DEC2003     31DEC2003
           1240060066      1         31AUG2006     31AUG2006
   ```

Level 2

2. Creating Macro Variables with the SYMPUTX Routine

a. Open the **m104e02** program shown below into the Editor window. This program creates a summary data set named `customer_sum` that summarizes `Total_Retail_Price` by `Customer_ID` and sorts the data set by descending `CustTotalPurchase`. Submit the program (part a) and examine the output that it creates.

```
proc means data=orion.order_fact nway noprint;
   var Total_Retail_Price;
   class Customer_ID;
   output out=customer_sum sum=CustTotalPurchase;
run;

proc sort data=customer_sum;
   by descending CustTotalPurchase;
run;

proc print data=customer_sum(drop=_type_);
run;
```

b. Create a macro variable named TOP that contains the ID number for the top customer. Then modify the program (part b) to print only the orders for Orion's top customer.

Partial PROC PRINT Output

```
            Orders for Customer 16 - Orion's Top Customer


                           Order_      Order_      Delivery_
              Order_ID      Type        Date        Date


              1230450371      2        24MAR2003   26MAR2003
              1231305521      2        27AUG2003   04SEP2003
              1231305531      2        27AUG2003   29AUG2003
              1234538390      2        12JAN2005   14JAN2005
              1234588648      2        17JAN2005   19JAN2005
```

c. Modify the program to print the customer's name instead of the customer's ID in the TITLE statement. Customer names are found in the **orion.customer_dim** data set.

Partial PROC PRINT Output

```
         Orders for Customer Ulrich Heyde - Orion's Top Customer


                           Order_      Order_      Delivery_
              Order_ID      Type        Date        Date


              1230450371      2        24MAR2003   26MAR2003
              1231305521      2        27AUG2003   04SEP2003
              1231305531      2        27AUG2003   29AUG2003
              1234538390      2        12JAN2005   14JAN2005
```

Level 3

3. Creating Macro Variables with the SYMPUTX Routine

a. Open the **m104e03** program shown below into the Editor window. Submit the program and examine the output that it creates.

```
proc means data=orion.order_fact nway noprint;
   var Total_Retail_Price;
   class Customer_ID;
   output out=customer_sum sum=CustTotalPurchase;
run;

proc sort data=customer_sum ;
   by descending CustTotalPurchase;
run;

proc print data=customer_sum(drop=_type_);
run;
```

b. Using the **customer_sum** data set, create a single macro variable, TOP3, that contains the customer IDs of the top three customers by revenue.

✎   **Customer_ID** is a numeric variable.

c. Using the **orion.customer_dim** data set, print a listing of the top three customers.

PROC PRINT Output

Top 3 Customers		
Customer_ID	Customer_Name	Customer_Type
10	Karen Ballinger	Orion Club members high activity
16	Ulrich Heyde	Internet/Catalog Customers
45	Dianne Patchin	Orion Club Gold members low activity

4.2   Indirect References to Macro Variables

Objectives

- Reference macro variables indirectly.
- Create a series of macro variables using the SYMPUTX routine.

38

Table Lookup Application

Example: Create an order history for a given customer.
Report titles should display customer name
and number.

```
                    Customer Number: 9
                 Customer Name: Cornelia Krahl

              Order_    Order_                   Total_Retail_
      Obs     Date      Type     Quantity        Price

      160     15APR2004    3          1              $29.40
      273     07JUN2005    3          2              $16.00
      288     10AUG2005    3          3           $1,542.60
      289     10AUG2005    3          2             $550.20
      316     02DEC2005    3          2              $39.20
      326     25DEC2005    3          1             $514.20
```

39

Table Lookup Application

Step 1: Hardcode the program, including customer name
and number.

```
proc print data=orion.order_fact;
   where customer_ID=9;
   var order_date order_type quantity total_retail_price;
   title1 "Customer Number: 9";
   title2 "Customer Name: Cornelia Krahl";
run;
```

40   m104d03a

Table Lookup Application

Step 2: Create and reference a macro variable for the
        customer number.

```
%let custID=9;
proc print data=orion.order_fact;
   where customer_ID=&custID;
   var order_date order_type quantity total_retail_price;
   title1 "Customer Number: &custID";
   title2 "Customer Name: Cornelia Krahl";
run;
```

How can you reference the customer name in TITLE2
without hardcoding it?

m104d03b

41

Table Lookup Application

The **orion.customer** data set contains customer
names and ID numbers. Customer ID numbers are unique.

| | | Orion.Customer | | | Birth_ |
Obs	Customer_ID	Customer_Name	Country	Gender	Date
1	4	James Kvarniq	US	M	27JUN1974
2	5	Sandrina Stephano	US	F	09JUL1979
3	9	Cornelia Krahl	DE	F	27FEB1974
4	10	Karen Ballinger	US	F	18OCT1984
5	11	Elke Wallstab	DE	F	16AUG1974
6	12	David Black	US	M	12APR1969
7	13	Markus Sepke	DE	M	21JUL1988
8	16	Ulrich Heyde	DE	M	16JAN1939
9	17	Jimmie Evans	US	M	17AUG1954
10	18	Tonie Asmussen	US	M	02FEB1954
11	19	Oliver S. Füßling	DE	M	23FEB1964
12	20	Michael Dineley	US	M	17APR1959

42

Table Lookup Application

Step 3: Add a DATA step to create a macro variable with the customer's name. Reference the macro variable in TITLE2.

```
%let custID=9;

data _null_;
   set orion.customer;
   where customer_ID=&custID;
   call symputx('name', Customer_Name);
run;

proc print data=orion.order_fact;
   where customer_ID=&custID;
   var order_date order_type quantity total_retail_price;
   title1 "Customer Number: &custID";
   title2 "Customer Name: &name";
run;
```

same statement

43   m104d03c

4.03 Quiz

How many rows are selected by the DATA step WHERE
statement in the preceding program, repeated below?

```
%let custID=9;
data _null_;
   set orion.customer;
   where customer_ID=&custID;
   call symputx('name', Customer_Name);
run;
proc print data=orion.order_fact;
   where customer_ID=&custID;
   var order_date order_type quantity total_retail_price;
   title1 "Customer Number: &custID";
   title2 "Customer Name: &name";
run;
```

m104d03c

45

Table Lookup Application

To select **all** customers, eliminate the WHERE statement
from the DATA step.

```
%let custID=9;
data _null_;
   set orion.customer;
   call symputx('name', Customer_Name);
run;
proc print data=orion.order_fact;
   where customer_ID=&custID;
   var order_date order_type quantity total_retail_price;
   title1 "Customer Number: &custID";
   title2 "Customer Name: &name";
run;
```

What is the problem this time?

47

Table Lookup Application

Because only one macro variable is created by the SYMPUTX routine, its value is overwritten with each iteration of the DATA step. Unique macro variable names are required.

```
%let custID=9;
data _null_;
   set orion.customer;
   call symputx('name', Customer_Name);
run;
proc print data=orion.order_fact;
   where customer_ID=&custID;
   var order_date order_type quantity total_retail_price;
   title1 "Customer Number: &custID";
   title2 "Customer Name: &name";
run;
```

48

Creating a Series of Macro Variables

Derive unique macro variable names by appending the Customer ID number to a fixed prefix.

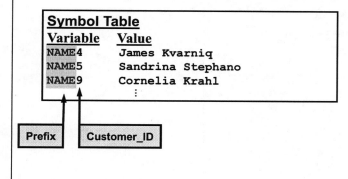

Symbol Table	
Variable	**Value**
NAME4	James Kvarniq
NAME5	Sandrina Stephano
NAME9	Cornelia Krahl
⋮	

Prefix   Customer_ID

49

Creating a Series of Macro Variables

To create a series of macro variables, use the SYMPUTX routine with a DATA step variable or expression in *argument1*.

CALL SYMPUTX(*expression1***,***expression2***);**

expression1 evaluates to a character value that is a valid macro variable name, unique to each execution of the routine.

expression2 is the value to assign to each macro variable.

50

Creating a Series of Macro Variables

Step 4: Create a series of macro variables to store customer names.

```
data _null_;
   set orion.customer;
   call symputx('name'||left(Customer_ID),
                customer_Name);
run;
```

m104d03d

51

Creating a Series of Macro Variables

Partial SAS Log

```
1276  %put _user_;
GLOBAL NAME61 Carsten Maestrini
GLOBAL NAME90 Kyndal Hooks
GLOBAL NAME1684 Carglar Aydemir
GLOBAL NAME12386 Avinoam Zweig
GLOBAL NAME9 Cornelia Krahl
GLOBAL NAME60 Tedi Lanzarone
GLOBAL NAME71 Viola Folsom
GLOBAL NAME2550 Sanelisiwe Collier
GLOBAL NAME11171 Bill Cuddy
GLOBAL NAME70210 Alex Santinello
GLOBAL NAME41 Wendell Summersby
GLOBAL NAME63 James Klisurich
GLOBAL NAME92 Lendon Celii
GLOBAL NAME19873 Avinoam Tuvia
GLOBAL NAME70201 Angel Borwick
GLOBAL NAME544 Avni Argac
GLOBAL NAME4 James Kvarniq
GLOBAL NAME50 Gert-Gunter Mendler
GLOBAL NAME65 Ines Deisser
```

52

Creating a Series of Macro Variables

You can now reference the correct name without re-running the DATA step.

Symbol Table	
Variable	**Value**
CUSTID	9
NAME4	James Kvarniq
NAME5	Sandrina Stephano
NAME9	Cornelia Krahl
⋮	⋮

```
%let custID=9;
proc print data=orion.order_fact;
   where customer_ID=&custID;
   var order_date order_type quantity total_retail_price;
   title1 "Customer Number: &custID";
   title2 "Customer Name: &name9";
run;
```

53

m104d03e

4.04 Quiz

Open program **m104a02**.

```
%let custID=9;
proc print data=orion.order_fact;
   where customer_ID=&custID;
   var order_date order_type quantity total_retail_price;
   title1 "Customer Number: &custID";
   title2 "Customer Name: &name9";
run;
```

Create an order history for CUSTID4.

How many program changes are required?

55

Indirect References to Macro Variables

Because the CUSTID macro variable matches **part of** the name of a NAME macro variable, the CUSTID macro variable can **indirectly reference** a NAME macro variable.

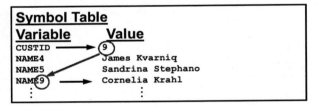

57

Indirect References to Macro Variables

The Forward Rescan Rule

- Multiple ampersands preceding a name token denote an indirect reference.
- Two ampersands (&&) resolve to one ampersand (&).
- The macro processor will rescan an indirect reference, left to right, from the point where multiple ampersands begin.
- Scanning continues until no more references can be resolved.

58

Indirect References to Macro Variables

Step 5: Use an indirect reference.

```
%let custID=9;
proc print data=orion.order_fact;
   where customer_ID=&custID;
   var order_date order_type quantity total_retail_price;
   title1 "Customer Number: &custID";
   title2 "Customer Name: &&name&custID";
run;
```

59   m104d03f

Indirect References to Macro Variables

The indirect reference causes a second scan.

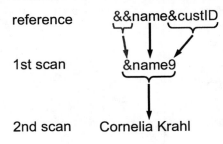

reference   &&name&custID

1st scan   &name9

2nd scan   Cornelia Krahl

60

Indirect References to Macro Variables

The CUSTID macro variable is an **indirect reference**
to a NAME macro variable.

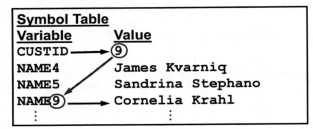

Symbol Table	
Variable	**Value**
CUSTID	9
NAME4	James Kvarniq
NAME5	Sandrina Stephano
NAME9	Cornelia Krahl
⋮	⋮

Scan sequence:

&&name&custID ⟶ &name9 ⟶ Cornelia Krahl

61

Indirect References to Macro Variables

PROC PRINT Output

```
                    Customer Number: 9
               Customer Name: Cornelia Krahl

              Order_     Order_                    Total_Retail_
      Obs      Date       Type     Quantity           Price

      160    15APR2004      3          1              $29.40
      273    07JUN2005      3          2              $16.00
      288    10AUG2005      3          3           $1,542.60
      289    10AUG2005      3          2             $550.20
      316    02DEC2005      3          2              $39.20
      326    25DEC2005      3          1             $514.20
```

62

4.05 Quiz

Submit program **m104a03**.

```
%let custid=9;
%let name9=Joe;
%put &name&custid;
```

How many times will the macro variables be scanned in
the %PUT statement?

Will this be successful?

64

Indirect References to Macro Variables

m104d03d, m104d03f

```
data _null_;
   set orion.customer;
   call symputx('name'||left(Customer_ID), customer_Name);
run;

%let custID=9;
proc print data=orion.order_fact;
   where customer_ID=&custID;
   var order_date order_type quantity total_retail_price;
   title1 "Customer Number: &custID";
   title2 "Customer Name: &&name&custID";
run;
```

Partial SAS Log

```
451   %let custID=9;
452   proc print data=orion.order_fact;
453       where customer_ID=&custID;
SYMBOLGEN:  Macro variable CUSTID resolves to 9
454       var order_date order_type quantity total_retail_price;
SYMBOLGEN:  Macro variable CUSTID resolves to 9
455       title1 "Customer Number: &custID";
SYMBOLGEN:  && resolves to &.
SYMBOLGEN:  Macro variable CUSTID resolves to 9
SYMBOLGEN:  Macro variable NAME9 resolves to Cornelia Krahl
456       title2 "Customer Name: &&name&custID";
457   run;

NOTE: There were 6 observations read from the data set ORION.ORDER_FACT.
      WHERE customer_ID=9;
NOTE: PROCEDURE PRINT used (Total process time):
      real time           0.01 seconds
      cpu time            0.00 seconds
```

PROC PRINT Output

```
                    Customer Number: 9
                 Customer Name: Cornelia Krahl


                  Order_    Order_                Total_Retail_
          Obs     Date      Type      Quantity        Price

          160     15APR2004    3          1          $29.40
          273     07JUN2005    3          2          $16.00
          288     10AUG2005    3          3       $1,542.60
          289     10AUG2005    3          2         $550.20
          316     02DEC2005    3          2          $39.20
          326     25DEC2005    3          1         $514.20
```

Indirect References to Macro Variables (Self-Study)

m104d03g

Three ampersands are sometimes required.

Example: Create a series of macro variables.

```
data _null_;
   set orion.country;
   call symputx(Country,country_name);
run;
```

SAS Log

```
771  %put _user_;
GLOBAL CA Canada
GLOBAL IL Israel
GLOBAL TR Turkey
GLOBAL AU Australia
GLOBAL US United States
GLOBAL DE Germany
GLOBAL ZA South Africa
```

Use a direct reference and an indirect reference.

```
%macro report(location=);
   proc print data=orion.customer;
      where Country="&location";
      title "Customers from &&&location";
   run;
%mend report;
```

SAS Log

```
784  %report(location=AU)
MPRINT(REPORT):    proc print data=orion.customer;
MPRINT(REPORT):    where Country="AU";
MPRINT(REPORT):    var Customer_ID Customer_Name Gender birth_date Country;
MPRINT(REPORT):    title "Customers from Australia";
MPRINT(REPORT):    run;
NOTE: There were 8 observations read from the data set ORION.CUSTOMER.
      WHERE Country='AU';
NOTE: PROCEDURE PRINT used (Total process time):
      real time           0.01 seconds
      cpu time            0.01 seconds
```

Apply the forward rescan rule: &&&location → &AU → Australia

Exercises

Level 1

4. **Creating Multiple Macro Variables with the SYMPUTX Routine**

   a. Open the **m104e04** program shown below into the Editor window.

```
%macro memberlist(id=1020);
   %put _user_;
   title "A List of &id";
   proc print data=orion.customer;
      var Customer_Name Customer_ID Gender;
      where Customer_Type_ID=&id;
   run;
%mend memberlist;


%memberlist()
```

   b. The **orion.customer_type** data set contains the variable **Customer_Type_ID**, which uniquely identifies the customer membership level and activity level. Modify the macro to include a DATA step to create a series of macro variables named TYPE*xxxx*, where *xxxx* is the value of **Customer_Type_ID**. The value of each TYPE macro variable should be the value of **Customer_Type**.

   Listing of **orion.customer_type**

	Customer_Type_ID	Customer_Type	Customer_Group	Customer_Group
1	1010	Orion Club members inactive	10	Orion Club members
2	1020	Orion Club members low activity	10	Orion Club members
3	1030	Orion Club members medium activity	10	Orion Club members
4	1040	Orion Club members high activity	10	Orion Club members
5	2010	Orion Club Gold members low activity	20	Orion Club Gold members
6	2020	Orion Club Gold members medium activity	20	Orion Club Gold members
7	2030	Orion Club Gold members high activity	20	Orion Club Gold members
8	3010	Internet/Catalog Customers	30	Internet/Catalog Customers

VIEWTABLE: Customer Type

c. Modify the TITLE statement so that it displays the appropriate customer type. Use an indirect macro variable reference to one of the TYPE variables based on the current value of ID. Submit the modified program.

Partial PROC PRINT Output

```
            A List of Orion Club members low activity

     Obs       Customer_Name        Customer_ID      Gender

      1        James Kvarniq              4            M
     10        Tonie Asmussen            18            M
     19        Alvan Goheen              34            M
```

d. Call the macro again, but with a parameter value of 2030.

Partial PROC PRINT Output

```
          A List of Orion Club Gold members high activity

     Obs       Customer_Name        Customer_ID      Gender

     11        Oliver S. Füßling         19            M
     21        Alphone Greenwald         39            M
     25        Annmarie Leveille         49            F
     26        Gert-Gunter Mendler       50            M
```

Level 2

5. Using Indirect References in a Macro Call

a. Open the **m104e05** program shown below into the Editor window. Submit the program and examine the results.

```
data _null_;
   set orion.customer_type;
   call symputx('type'||left(Customer_Type_ID), Customer_Type);
run;

%put _user_;

%macro memberlist(custtype);
   proc print data=orion.customer_dim;
      var Customer_Name Customer_ID Customer_Age_Group;
      where Customer_Type="&custtype";
      title "A List of &custtype";
   run;
%mend memberlist;
```

b. Create a macro variable named NUM with the value `2010`. Call the MEMBERLIST macro. Pass the appropriate parameter to the MEMBERLIST macro, such that CUSTTYPE resolves to `Orion Club members low activity` on the macro call.

PROC PRINT Output

```
              A List of Orion Club Gold members low activity

                                                   Customer_
         Obs    Customer_Name       Customer_ID    Age_Group

          7     Markus Sepke                 13     15-30 years
         24     Dianne Patchin               45     15-30 years
         53     Sanelisiwe Collier         2550     15-30 years
         58     Bill Cuddy                11171     15-30 years
         75     Angel Borwick             70201     31-45 years
```

Level 3

6. Using a Table Lookup Application

a. Using `orion.country`, create a series of macro variables in which the name of the macro variable is the country abbreviation (**Country**) and the value of the macro variable is the country name (**Country_Name**).

b. Open the **m104e06** program shown below into the Editor window.

```
%let code=AU;
proc print data=Orion.Employee_Addresses;
   var Employee_Name City;
   where Country="&code";
   title "A List of xxxxx Employees";
run;
```

c. Use indirect macro variable referencing to replace the **xxxxx** with the appropriate country name.

Partial PROC PRINT Output

```
                     A List of Australia Employees

         Obs     Employee_Name          City

          2     Aisbitt, Sandy          Melbourne
         17     Bahlman, Sharon         Sydney
         18     Baker, Gabriele         Sydney
         22     Baran, Shanmuganathan   Sydney
         23     Barbis, Viney           Sydney
         24     Barcoe, Selina          Melbourne
         25     Barreto, Geok-Seng      Sydney
         31     Billington, Kareen      Sydney
         34     Blanton, Brig           Melbourne
         37     Body, Meera             Sydney
         48     Buddery, Jeannette      Sydney
         52     Cantatore, Lorian       Sydney
```

4.3 Retrieving Macro Variables in the DATA Step (Self-Study)

Objectives

- Obtain the value of a macro variable during DATA step execution.
- Describe the difference between the SYMGET function and macro variable references.

70

The SYMGET Function

	create macro variables	retrieve macro variables
word scanning time	%LET	&macvar
execution time	CALL SYMPUTX	SYMGET(macvar)

75

The SYMGET Function

Retrieve a macro variable's value during DATA step execution with the SYMGET function.

Program Data Vector

| DATA Step Variables | ←—SYMGET—— | Symbol Table |

76

The SYMGET Function

General form of the SYMGET function:

> **SYMGET(**macro-variable**)**

macro-variable can be specified as either of the following:
- character literal
- DATA step character expression

A DATA step variable created by the SYMGET function is a character variable with a length of 200 bytes **unless it has been previously defined**.

77

Review

Create a series of macro variables to store customer names.

```
data _null_;
   set orion.customer;
   call symputx('name'||left(customer_ID),
                customer_name);
run;
```

Symbol Table	
name4	James Kvarniq
name5	Sandrina Stephano
name9	Cornelia Krahl

78   m104d03d

The SYMGET Function

Example: Look up customer names from the symbol table.

```
data InternetCustomers;
   keep order_date customer_ID customer_name;
   set orion.order_fact;
   if order_type=3;
   length Customer_Name $ 20;
   Customer_Name=symget('name'||left(customer_ID));
run;

proc print data=InternetCustomers;
   var order_date customer_ID customer_name;
   title "Internet Customers";
run;
```

m104d04

79

The SYMGET Function

Partial PROC PRINT Output

```
                      Internet Customers

              Order_
   Obs          Date    Customer_ID    Customer_Name

    1        02APR2003        70046     Tommy Mcdonald
    2        18APR2003           36     Phenix Hill
    3        01MAY2003          171     Robert Bowerman
    4        07MAY2003        11171     Bill Cuddy
    5        20JUN2003        17023     Susan Krasowski
    6        20JUN2003        17023     Susan Krasowski
    7        03JUL2003          171     Robert Bowerman
    8        15JUL2003           36     Phenix Hill
    9        15JUL2003           36     Phenix Hill
   10        06AUG2003         3959     Rita Lotz
   11        06AUG2003         3959     Rita Lotz
   12        20AUG2003           52     Yan Kozlowski
```

80

 **Exercises**

Level 1

7. Resolving Macro Variables with the SYMGET Function

a. Open the **m104e07** program shown below into the Editor window to create a series of macro variables containing the customer type. Submit the first DATA step and the %PUT statement and examine the results.

```
data _null_;
   set orion.customer_type;
   call symputx('type'||left(Customer_Type_ID), Customer_Type);
run;

%put _user_;

data us;
   set orion.customer;
   where Country="US";
   keep Customer_ID Customer_Name Customer_Type_ID;
run;

proc print data=us noobs;
   title "US Customers";
run;
```

b. Modify the second DATA step to create a new variable named **CustType** that contains the value of the macro variable TYPE*xxxx* created in part **a**. Add the new variable to the KEEP statement.

Partial PROC PRINT Output

			US Customers	

Customer_ID	Customer_Name	Customer_Type_ID	CustType
4	James Kvarniq	1020	Orion Club members low activity
5	Sandrina Stephano	2020	Orion Club Gold members medium activity
10	Karen Ballinger	1040	Orion Club members high activity
12	David Black	1030	Orion Club members medium activity
17	Jimmie Evans	1030	Orion Club members medium activity
18	Tonie Asmussen	1020	Orion Club members low activity
20	Michael Dineley	1030	Orion Club members medium activity
23	Tulio Devereaux	3010	Internet/Catalog Customers
24	Robyn Klem	3010	Internet/Catalog Customers
27	Cynthia Mccluney	3010	Internet/Catalog Customers
31	Cynthia Martinez	2020	Orion Club Gold members medium activity
34	Alvan Goheen	1020	Orion Club members low activity
36	Phenix Hill	3010	Internet/Catalog Customers

Level 2

8. Investigating Macro Variable Storage and Resolution

Determine the type, length, and value of the DATA step variables in the program below.

```
%let var1=cat;
%let var2=3;
data test;
    length s1 s4 s5 $ 3;
    call symputx('var3','dog');
    r1="&var1";
    r2=&var2;
    r3="&var3";
    s1=symget('var1');
    s2=symget('var2');
    s3=input(symget('var2'),2.);
    s4=symget('var3');
    s5=symget('var'||left(r2));
run;
```

Name	Type	Length	Value
R1			
R2			
R3			
S1			
S2			
S3			
S4			
S5			

Hint: Mimic SAS processing by making **two** passes through the program:
a word-scanning/compilation pass and an execution pass.

Hint: Draw a symbol table, updating it as each macro variable is created and populated.

4.4 Creating Macro Variables in SQL

Objectives

- Create macro variables during PROC SQL execution.
- Store several values in one macro variable using the SQL procedure.

[handwritten note:]

```
proc sql noprint;
  select name into :
  names separated
  by ',' from ss.help;
quit;  %put &names
```

84

The SQL Procedure INTO Clause

The INTO clause creates macro variables.

General form of the SQL procedure INTO clause:

```
SELECT col1, col2, . . . INTO :mvar1, :mvar2,...
    FROM table-expression
    WHERE where-expression
    ORDER BY col1, col2, . . . ;
```

This form of the INTO clause does not trim leading or trailing blanks.

85

A %LET statement can be used to trim leading and trailing blanks created by the INTO clause:

```
%let macrovariable=&macrovariable;
```

The SQL Procedure INTO Clause

Example: Create a macro variable that contains the
total price of all 2007 Internet orders.

```
proc sql noprint;
    select sum(total_retail_price) format=dollar8.
        into : total
        from orion.order_fact
        where year(order_date)=2007 and order_type=3;
quit;
```

Partial SAS Log

```
1451   %put Total 2007 Internet Sales: &total;
Total 2007 Internet Sales:    $6,731
```

m104d05a

86

The SQL Procedure INTO Clause

The INTO clause can create multiple macro variables.

Example: Create macro variables with the date and
amount of the top three sales from 2007.

```
title 'Top 2007 Sales';
proc sql outobs=3 double;
   select total_retail_price, order_date format=mmddyy10.
      into :price1-:price3, :date1-:date3
      from orion.order_fact
      where year(order_date)=2007
      order by total_retail_price desc;
quit;
```

87   m104d05b

The SQL Procedure INTO Clause

SQL Result

Top 2007 Sales	
Total_Retail_Price	Order_Date
$1,937.20	06/20/2007
$1,066.40	11/01/2007
$760.80	12/12/2007

Macro variables
PRICE1⇨
PRICE2⇨
PRICE3⇨

Macro variables
⇦DATE1
⇦DATE2
⇦DATE3

Partial SAS Log

```
1529   %put &price1 &date1, &price2 &date2, &price3 &date3;
$1,937.20 06/20/2007, $1,066.40 11/01/2007, $760.80 12/12/2007
```

88   m104d05b

The SQL Procedure INTO Clause

The INTO clause can store the unique values of a specified column in a single macro variable.

General form of the INTO clause to create a list of unique values in one macro variable:

SELECT DISTINCT *col1*, . . .
    INTO :*mvar* SEPARATED BY '*delimiter*', . . .
    FROM *table-expression*
    WHERE *where-expression*
    other clauses;

89

The SQL Procedure INTO Clause

Example: Create a macro variable with a list of all customer countries. Delimit the country codes with a comma and a space.

```
proc sql noprint;
   select distinct country into :countries
       separated by ', '
       from orion.customer;
quit;
```

Partial SAS Log

```
1550  %put Customer Countries: &Countries;
Customer Countries: AU, CA, DE, IL, TR, US, ZA
```

m104d05c

90

The DATA step below creates the same macro variable.

```
proc sort data=orion.customer(keep=country) nodupkey out=allcountries;
   by country;
run;

data _null_;
   set allcountries end=eof;
   length countries $ 50;
   retain countries;
   countries=catx(', ', countries, country);
   if eof then call symputx('countries', countries);
run;
```

%put &sqlobs;
to get # of obs if
using price1 to price999

4.06 Multiple Choice Poll

Which technique creates macro variables during execution time?

a. %LET statement

b. SYMPUTX routine

c. INTO clause

d. Both b and c

92

Review

Example: Display user-defined macro variables.

SAS Log

```
662  %put _user_;
GLOBAL SQLOBS 7
GLOBAL SQLOOPS 100
GLOBAL PRICE1 $1,937.20
GLOBAL MONTH 1
GLOBAL CUSTID 9
GLOBAL SYS_SQL_IP_ALL 0
GLOBAL DATE1 06/20/2007
GLOBAL COUNTRIES AU, CA, DE, IL, TR, US, ZA
GLOBAL DAT 01/28/2007
GLOBAL DATE2 11/01/2007
GLOBAL YEAR 2007
GLOBAL TOTAL    $6,731
GLOBAL DATE3 12/12/2007
GLOBAL NAME Cornelia Krahl
GLOBAL ORDERS 148
GLOBAL START 01Jan2007
GLOBAL SQLXOBS 0
GLOBAL SQLRC 0
GLOBAL AVG $125
GLOBAL STOP 31Dec2007
GLOBAL AVERAGE 157.49094595
GLOBAL SQLEXITCODE 0
GLOBAL PRICE2 $1,066.40
GLOBAL PRICE3 $760.80
```

94

The SQL Procedure

Example: Display user-defined macro variables alphabetically.

```
proc sql flow;
    select name, value
        from dictionary.macros
        where scope='GLOBAL'
        order by name;
quit;
```

95   m104d05d

The `dictionary.macros` table is one of several PROC SQL read-only DICTIONARY tables that store SAS metadata. For additional information, see "Accessing SAS System Information Using DICTIONARY Tables" under "Programming with the SQL Procedure" in the *SQL Procedure User's Guide*.

The SQL Procedure

PROC SQL Output

```
Macro Variable
Name              Macro Variable Value

AVERAGE           157.49094595
AVG               $125
COUNTRIES         AU, CA, DE, IL, TR, US, ZA
CUSTID            9
DAT               01/28/2007
DATE1             06/20/2007
DATE2             11/01/2007
DATE3             12/12/2007
MONTH             1
NAME              Cornelia Krahl
ORDERS            148
PRICE1            $1,937.20
PRICE2            $1,066.40
PRICE3            $760.80
SQLEXITCODE       0
SQLOBS            0
SQLOOPS           0
SQLRC             0
SQLXOBS           0
START             01Jan2007
STOP              31Dec2007
SYS_SQL_IP_ALL    0
TOTAL                $6,731
YEAR              2007
```

96

The SQL Procedure

Example: Create a utility macro to display user-defined
macro variables alphabetically.

```
%macro putALL;
   proc sql flow;
      select name, value
         from dictionary.macros
         where scope='GLOBAL'
         order by name;
   quit;
%mend putALL;
```

Call the macro:

```
%putALL
```

m104d05d

97

The SQL Procedure INTO Clause

Example: Create a macro variable with a list of all
user-defined macro variable names. Delimit
the names with spaces.

```
proc sql noprint;
   select name into: vars separated by ' '
      from dictionary.macros
      where scope='GLOBAL';
quit;
```

describe
dictionary.macros

Partial SAS Log

```
705  %put &vars;
SQLOBS SQLOOPS PRICE1 MONTH CUSTID SYS_SQL_IP_ALL DATE1 COUNTRIES
DAT DATE2 YEAR TOTAL DATE3 NAME ORDERS START SQLXOBS SQLRC AVG STOP
AVERAGE SQLEXITCODE PRICE2 PRICE3
```

98

The SQL Procedure INTO Clause

Example: Create a utility macro that deletes all user-defined
macro variables.

```
%macro deleteALL;

   proc sql noprint;
     select name into: vars separated by ' '
        from dictionary.macros
        where scope='GLOBAL';
   quit;

   %symdel &vars;

%mend deleteALL;

%deleteALL
```

99   m104d05e

Exercises

Level 1

9. Creating Macro Variables Using SQL

   a. Open the **m104e09** program shown below into the Editor window.

```
%let start=01Jan2007;
%let stop=31Jan2007;

proc means data=orion.order_fact noprint;
   where order_date between "&start"d and "&stop"d;
   var Quantity Total_Retail_Price;
   output out=stats mean=Avg_Quant Avg_Price;
   run;

data _null_;
   set stats;
   call symputx('Quant',put(Avg_Quant,4.2));
   call symputx('Price',put(Avg_Price,dollar7.2));
run;

proc print data=orion.order_fact noobs n;
   where order_date between "&start"d and "&stop"d;
   var Order_ID Order_Date Quantity Total_Retail_Price;
   sum Quantity Total_Retail_Price;
   format Total_Retail_Price dollar6.;
   title1 "Report from &start to &stop";
   title3 "Average Quantity: &quant";
   title4 "Average Price: &price";
run;
```

b. Submit the program and view the results.

```
                    Report from 01Jan2007 to 31Jan2007

                          Average Quantity: 2.15
                          Average Price: $173.89


                                                   Total_
                                   Order_          Retail_
                Order_ID            Date   Quantity  Price

                1241054779        02JAN2007     2     $196
                1241063739        03JAN2007     6     $161
                1241066216        04JAN2007     2     $306
                1241086052        06JAN2007     3      $38
                1241147641        13JAN2007     2     $363
                1241235281        23JAN2007     1      $73
                1241244297        24JAN2007     2     $258
                1241244297        24JAN2007     2      $81
                1241244297        24JAN2007     3     $358
                1241263172        25JAN2007     1     $102
                1241263172        25JAN2007     1     $113
                1241286432        28JAN2007     2     $174
                1241298131        29JAN2007     1      $37
                                             ========  =======
                                               28     $2,261

                              N = 13
```

c. Delete the macro variables QUANT and PRICE.

d. Replace the PROC MEANS step and the DATA step with a PROC SQL step.

e. Resubmit the PROC PRINT step and verify that the output is the same.

Level 2

10. Creating a List of Values in a Macro Variable Using SQL

a. Open the **m104e10** program into the Editor window. Create a macro variable named TOP3 with the customer ID numbers of the top three customers by **Total_Retail_Price**. Separate the ID numbers with a comma and a blank. Use the OUTOBS= option.

```
proc sql;
   select customer_id, sum(Total_Retail_Price) as total
      from orion.order_fact
      group by Customer_ID
      order by total descending;
quit;
```

> 🖋 The GROUP BY clause summarizes the data by customer ID number.
>
> The ORDER BY clause sorts the data in descending order.

b. Submit the program and review the results, which are shown below.

```
                          Top 3 Customers

         Customer_ID     Customer_Name         Customer_Type

                  10     Karen Ballinger    Orion  Club members high activity
                  16     Ulrich Heyde       Internet/Catalog Customers
                  45     Dianne Patchin     Orion Club Gold members low activity
```

Level 3

11. Creating Multiple Macro Variables Using SQL

a. The **orion.customer_type** data set contains the variable **Customer_Type_ID**, which holds the unique customer type codes. Use the SQL procedure to create a series of macro variables named CTYPE1 through CTYPE*xx*, where *xx* resolves to the number of rows that the query will return.

> You will need two queries, one to return the number of rows that the query will return and the other to create CTYPE1 through CTYPE*xx*.

b. Open the program **m104e11** to display only the macro variables that begin with CTYPE.

```
proc sql;
   select name, value
      from dictionary.macros
      where name like "CTYPE%";
quit;
```

PROC SQL Output

Macro Variable beginning with CTYPE	
Macro Variable Name	Macro Variable Value
CTYPE1	1010
CTYPE2	1020
CTYPE3	1030
CTYPE8	3010
CTYPE4	1040
CTYPE5	2010
CTYPE6	2020
CTYPE7	2030

4.5 Chapter Review

Chapter Review

1. What statement creates macro variables in the
    DATA step?

2. What values are available to the SYMPUTX routine?

3. What is the difference between the SYMPUTX routine
    and the %LET statement?

102

Chapter Review

4. How is an indirect reference coded?

5. How do multiple ampersands resolve?

6. What SQL feature creates macro variables?

104

4.6 Solutions

Solutions to Exercises

1. **Creating Macro Variables with the SYMPUTX Routine**

   a. Open the program into the Editor window.

   b. Modify the macro to include a DATA step that creates a macro variable named NAME based on the variable **Employee_Name** found in the **orion.employee_addesses** data set.

   c. Modify the TITLE statement to display the name of the employee instead of the employee's ID number. Call the macro using the default parameter value.

   ```
   %macro emporders(idnum=121044);
      data _null_;
         set orion.employee_addresses;
         where Employee_ID=&idnum;
         call symputx('name',Employee_Name);
      run;
      proc print data=orion.orders noobs;
         var Order_ID Order_Type Order_Date Delivery_Date;
         where Employee_ID=&idnum;
         title "Orders Taken by Employee &name";
      run;
   %mend emporders;

   %emporders()
   ```

   d. Call the macro again, but with a parameter value of `121066`.

   ```
   %emporders(idnum=121066)
   ```

2. Creating Macro Variables with the SYMPUTX Routine

a. Open the program into the Editor window.

b. Create a macro variable named TOP that contains the ID number of the top customer. Then modify the program (part b) to print only the orders for Orion's top customer.

```
data _null_;
   set customer_sum (obs=1);
   call symputx('top', Customer_ID);
run;

proc print data=orion.orders noobs;
   where Customer_ID =&top;
   var Order_ID Order_Type Order_Date Delivery_Date;
   title "Orders for Customer &top - Orion's Top Customer";
run;
```

c. Modify the program to print the customer's name instead of the customer's ID in the TITLE statement. Customer names are found in the **orion.customer_dim** data set.

```
data _null_;
   set customer_sum (obs=1);
   call symputx('top', Customer_ID);
run;

data _null_;
   set orion.customer_dim;
   where Customer_ID = &top;
   call symputx('topname', Customer_Name);
run;

proc print data=orion.orders noobs;
   where Customer_ID =&top;
   var Order_ID Order_Type Order_Date Delivery_Date;
   title "Orders for Customer &topname - Orion's Top Customer";
run;
```

3. Creating Macro Variables with the SYMPUTX Routine

a. Open the program into the Editor window.

b. Using the **customer_sum** data set, create the macro variable, TOP3, which contains the customer IDs of the top three customers by revenue.

```
data _null_;
   set customer_sum(obs=3) end=last;
   length top3 $50;
   retain top3;
   top3=catx(' ',top3, Customer_ID);
   /* Alternative Solution for the CATX Function    */
   /* top3=trim(top3)||' '||left(Customer_ID);      */
   if  last then call symputx('top3', top3);
run;
```

c. Using the **orion.customer_dim** data set, print a listing of the top three customers.

```
proc print data=orion.customer_dim noobs;
   where Customer_ID in (&top3);
   var Customer_ID Customer_Name Customer_Type;
   title 'Top 3 Customers';
run;
```

4. Creating Multiple Macro Variables with the SYMPUTX Routine

a. Open the program into the Editor window.

b. Concatenating the text **type** with the value of the **Customer_Type_ID** variable specifies the name of each macro variable. Because the **Customer_Type_ID** variable is numeric, the LEFT function is required to remove the leading blanks introduced by the automatic numeric-to-character conversion. The %PUT statement displays the names and values of all user-created macro variables.

c. Because each macro variable that contains the customer type has a common root at the start of its name (TYPE) and a suffix that corresponds to the value of the ID macro variable, two ampersands are used in front of the complete reference.

```
%macro memberlist(id=1020);
   data _null_;
     set orion.customer_type;
     call symputx('type'||left(Customer_Type_ID), Customer_Type);
     *Alternative Solution Using the CATS function               ;
     *call symputx(cats('type',Customer_Type_ID), Customer_Type);
   run;
   %put _user_;
   title "A List of &&type&id";
   proc print data=orion.customer;
     var Customer_Name Customer_ID Gender;
     where Customer_Type_ID=&id;
   run;
%mend memberlist;
%memberlist()
```

SAS Log

```
39    %put _user_;
GLOBAL TYPE1010 Orion Club members inactive
GLOBAL TYPE1020 Orion Club members low activity
GLOBAL TYPE2010 Orion Club Gold members low activity
GLOBAL TYPE1030 Orion  Club members medium activity
GLOBAL TYPE2020 Orion Club Gold members medium activity
GLOBAL TYPE3010 Internet/Catalog Customers
GLOBAL TYPE1040 Orion  Club members high activity
GLOBAL TYPE2030 Orion Club Gold members high activity

40    options symbolgen;
41    %let id=1020;
42    proc print data=orion.customer;
43        var Customer_Name Customer_ID Gender;
44        where Customer_Type_ID=&id;
SYMBOLGEN:  Macro variable ID resolves to 1020
SYMBOLGEN:  && resolves to &.
SYMBOLGEN:  Macro variable ID resolves to 1020
SYMBOLGEN:  Macro variable TYPE1020 resolves to Orion Club members low activity
45        title "A List of &&type&id";
46    run;

NOTE: There were 17 observations read from the data set ORION.CUSTOMER.
      WHERE Customer_Type_ID=1020;
NOTE: PROCEDURE PRINT used (Total process time):
      real time           0.17 seconds
      cpu time            0.00 seconds
```

d. Call the macro again, but with a parameter value of 2030.

```
%memberlist(id=2030)
```

Partial SAS Log

```
SYMBOLGEN:  && resolves to &.
SYMBOLGEN:  Macro variable ID resolves to 2030
SYMBOLGEN:  Macro variable TYPE2030 resolves to Orion Club Gold members high activity
SYMBOLGEN:  Macro variable ID resolves to 2030

NOTE: There were 10 observations read from the data set ORION.CUSTOMER.
      WHERE Customer_Type_ID=2030;
NOTE: PROCEDURE PRINT used (Total process time):
      real time           1.43 seconds
      cpu time            0.00 seconds
```

5. Using Indirect References in a Macro Call

a. Open the program into the Editor window.

b. Create a macro variable named NUM with the value of 2010. Execute the macro so that the value of CUSTTYPE resolves to Orion Club members low activity in the macro call.

```
%let num=2010;
%memberlist(&&type&num)
```

Partial SAS Log

```
18    %let num=2010;
19    %memberlist(&&type&num)
SYMBOLGEN:  && resolves to &.
SYMBOLGEN:  Macro variable NUM resolves to 2010
SYMBOLGEN:  Macro variable TYPE2010 resolves to Orion Club Gold members low activity
SYMBOLGEN:  Macro variable CUSTTYPE resolves to Orion Club Gold members low activity
SYMBOLGEN:  Macro variable CUSTTYPE resolves to Orion Club Gold members low activity
NOTE: There were 5 observations read from the data set ORION.CUSTOMER_DIM.
      WHERE Customer_Type='Orion Club Gold members low activity';
NOTE: PROCEDURE PRINT used (Total process time):
      real time           2.24 seconds
      cpu time            0.00 seconds
```

6. Using a Table Lookup Application

a. Using **orion.country**, create a series of macro variables in which the name of the macro variable is the country abbreviation (**Country**) and the value of the macro variable is the country name (**Country_Name**).

```
data _null_;
   set orion.country;
   call symputx(Country, Country_Name);
run;
%put _user_;
```

Partial SAS Log

```
7     %put _user_;
GLOBAL CA Canada
GLOBAL IL Israel
GLOBAL TR Turkey
GLOBAL AU Australia
GLOBAL US United States
GLOBAL DE Germany
GLOBAL ZA South Africa
```

b. Open the program into the Editor window.

c. Use indirect macro variable referencing to replace the **xxxxx** with the appropriate country name.

```
%let code=AU;
proc print data=orion.employee_addresses;
   var Employee_Name City;
   where Country="&code";
   title "A List of &&&code Employees";
run;
```

7. Resolving Macro Variables with the SYMGET Function

   a. Open the program into the Editor window.

   b. The correct customer type can be obtained by appending the value of **Customer_Type_ID** as a suffix to TYPE to identify the corresponding macro variable name.

```
data us;
   set orion.customer;
   where Country="US";
   CustType=symget("type"||left(Customer_Type_ID));
   keep Customer_ID Customer_Name Customer_Type_ID CustType;
run;
```

8. Investigating Macro Variable Storage and Resolution

Word Scanning

Substitutions based on macro variable references using & occur during word scanning.

R1 and **R2**   Macro variables VAR1 and VAR2 exist, so both substitutions occur.

R3   The macro variable VAR3 does not exist until the CALL SYMPUTX statement executes, so no substitution is made.

```
data test:
length s1 s4 s5 $ 3;
call symputx('var3','dog');
r1="cat";
r2=3;
r3="&var3";
s1=symget('var1');
s2=symget('var2');
s3=input(symget('var2'),2.);
s4=symget('var3');
s5=symget('var'||left(r2));
run;
```

Compilation

The attributes of each variable are determined during compilation of the resulting DATA step program:

```
data test:
length s1 s4 s5 $ 3;
call symputx('var3','dog');
r1="cat";
r2=3;
r3="&var3";
s1=symget('var1');
s2=symget('var2');
s3=input(symget('var2'),2.);
s4=symget('var3');
s5=symget('var'||left(r2));
run;
```

S1, S4, S5	Explicit definition as character variables with length 3.
R2	The lack of quotation marks around the assigned value indicates a numeric variable. Default length for numeric variables is 8.
R1 and **R3**	Quotation marks around the assigned value indicate a character variable. The number of characters inside the quotation marks determines the length.
S2	Assignment from the SYMGET function indicates a character variable. No explicitly assigned length defaults to 200; the compiler does not know what value will be in the symbol table during execution; and the 200 bytes are allocated.
S3	Assignment from the INPUT function with a numeric informat indicates a numeric variable. The default length for numeric variables is 8.

Execution

The values of each variable are determined during execution of the program. It is at this time that the CALL SYMPUTX statement creates the macro variable VAR3 so that its value is available for retrieval by the SYMGET function later in the DATA step.

R1 and **R2**   Hardcoded values are assigned.

R3   The reference &VAR3 is a text string during execution, so this is also a hardcoded value.

S1   The value is obtained from the symbol table.

S2   The value that is obtained from the symbol tables does not fill allotment of 200 characters; there are 199 trailing blanks.

S3   The first two characters that are obtained from the symbol table are converted into a numeric value using the 2. informat.

S4 and **S5**   The same value is obtained from the symbol table because each SYMGET argument results in the character string `var3`. The macro variable VAR3 was created earlier in the execution of the DATA step.

Name	Type	Length	Value
R1	Char	3	cat
R2	Num	8	3
R3	Char	5	&var3
S1	Char	3	cat
S2	Char	200	3
S3	Num	8	3
S4	Char	3	dog
S5	Char	3	dog

9. **Creating Macro Variables Using SQL**

  a. Open the program into the Editor window.

  b. Submit the program and view the results.

  c. Delete the macro variables QUANT and PRICE.

```
%symdel quant price;
```

  d. Replace the PROC MEANS step and the DATA step with a PROC SQL step.

```
proc sql noprint;
   select mean(Quantity) format=4.2,
          mean(Total_Retail_Price) format=dollar7.2
      into :quant, :price
      from orion.order_fact
      where order_date between "&start"d and "&stop"d;
quit;
```

  e. Resubmit the PROC PRINT step and verify that the output is the same.

10. **Creating a List of Values in a Macro Variable Using SQL**

  a. Open the **m104e10** program into the Editor window and modify the SQL procedure to create a macro variable named TOP3 that contains the customer ID numbers of the top three customers by **Total_Retail_Price** in the **orion.order_fact** data set. Separate each of the values with a comma and a blank. Use the OUTOBS= option to limit the number of output rows.

```
proc sql noprint outobs=3;
   select customer_id, sum(Total_Retail_Price) as total
          into :top3 separated by ', '
      from orion.order_fact
      group by Customer_ID
      order by total descending;
```

  b. Submit the program and review the results, which are shown in part **b** of the exercise.

11. **Creating Multiple Macro Variables Using SQL**

  a. The first query creates the NUMOBS macro variable that stores how many records will be returned by the query. This is the same as the number of macro variables in each series.

  A special form of the INTO clause is useful for creating a series of macro variables from multiple rows of an SQL query.

```
proc sql noprint;
   select count(*) into :numobs
      from orion.customer_type;
   %let numobs=&numobs;
   select Customer_Type_ID into :ctype1-:ctype&numobs
      from orion.customer_type;
quit;
```

  b. Submit the program and review the results, which are shown in part **b** of the exercise.

Solutions to Student Activities (Polls/Quizzes)

4.01 Multiple Choice Poll – Correct Answer

What is the value of FOOT after execution of the
DATA step?

```
data _null_;
   call symputx('foot','No internet orders');
   %let foot=Some internet orders;
run;
```

(a.) No internet orders
b. Some internet orders

1. **Word scanning begins. DATA step compilation begins.**
2. **%LET encountered. Macro trigger executes.**
3. **Step boundary. DATA step executes.**
   SYMPUTX executes.

20

4.02 Quiz – Correct Answer

Edit the CALL SYMPUTX routines to format values.

- Display DAT as a date such as 11/21/2009.
- Display AVG as a number with dollar signs and no decimal places.

```
call symputx('dat', put(date,mmddyy10.));
call symputx('avg', put(amount/number,dollar8.));
```

30

4.03 Quiz – Correct Answer

How many rows are selected by the DATA step using the WHERE statement in the program below?

One row

```
%let custID=9;
data _null_;
   set orion.customer;
   where customer_ID=&custID;
   call symputx('name', Customer_Name);
run;
proc print data=orion.order_fact;
   where customer_ID=&custID;
   var order_date order_type quantity total_retail_price;
   title1 "Customer Number: &custID";
   title2 "Customer Name: &name";
run;
```

Each time you select a customer number, the DATA step rereads the entire customer data set to select a subset of <u>one</u> customer.

46   m104d03c

4.04 Quiz – Correct Answer

How many program changes are required?

Two program changes are required.

```
%let custID=4;   ◄ Change
proc print data=orion.order_fact;
   where customer_ID=&custID;
   var order_date order_type quantity total_retail_price;
   title1 "Customer Number: &custID";
   title2 "Customer Name: &name4";   ◄ Change
run;
```

56

4.05 Quiz – Correct Answer

Submit program **m104a03**.

```
%let custid=9;
%let name9=Joe;
%put &name&custid;
```

How many times will the macro variables be scanned in the %PUT statement?

One time

Will this be successful?

No, it will generate the following warning:

```
WARNING: Apparent symbolic reference NAME not resolved.
```

65

4.06 Multiple Choice Poll – Correct Answer

Which technique creates macro variables during execution time?

a. %LET statement
b. SYMPUTX routine
c. INTO clause
d. Both b and c

93

Solutions to Chapter Review

Chapter Review – Correct Answers

1. What statement creates macro variables in the DATA step?

   CALL SYMPUTX

2. What values are available to the SYMPUTX routine?

   DATA step variables, expressions, and character literals

3. What is the difference between the SYMPUTX routine and the %LET statement?

   The SYMPUTX routine is a DATA step statement that works during DATA step execution time. The %LET statement is a macro trigger that works during word-scanning time.

103

Chapter Review – Correct Answers

4. How is an indirect reference coded?

   With multiple ampersands

5. How do multiple ampersands resolve?

   Two ampersands resolve to one ampersand

6. What SQL feature creates macro variables?

   The INTO clause

105

Chapter 5   Macro Programs

5.1   **Conditional Processing** **5-3**

      Exercises 5-18

5.2   **Parameter Validation** **5-20**

      Exercises 5-27

5.3   **Iterative Processing** **5-30**

      Exercises 5-45

5.4   **Global and Local Symbol Tables**...**5-48**

      Exercises 5-66

5.5   **Chapter Review**..**5-70**

5.6   **Solutions** **5-71**

      Solutions to Exercises 5-71

      Solutions to Student Activities (Polls/Quizzes) 5-84

      Solutions to Chapter Review 5-88

5.1 Conditional Processing

Objectives

- Conditionally process SAS code within a macro program.
- Monitor macro execution.
- Insert entire steps, entire statements, and partial statements into a SAS program.

3

Macro-Level Programming

Macro-level programming can generate code conditionally.
Conditions can be based on the following:

- system values
- parameter values
- data values

Example: Orion Star submits a program every night to
report daily sales. Every Friday, a second
program is submitted to summarize weekly
sales.

Automate the application so that only **one
program** is required.

4

Macro-Level Programming

Always print
the
daily report

```
proc print data=orion.order_fact;
    where order_date="&sysdate9"d;
    var product_id total_retail_price;
    title "Daily sales: &sysdate9";
run;
```

Is it
Friday?   Yes

```
proc means data=orion.order_fact n sum mean;
    where order_date between
          "&sysdate9"d - 6 and "&sysdate9"d;
    var quantity total_retail_price;
    title "Weekly sales: &sysdate9";
run;
```

5

Conditional Processing

Conditional processing is performed with %IF-%THEN and %ELSE statements.

General form of %IF-%THEN and %ELSE statements:

> **%IF** *expression* **%THEN** *action*;
> **%ELSE** *action*;

expression   can be any valid macro expression.

The %ELSE statement is optional.

These macro language statements can be used only inside a macro definition.

6

Macro Expressions

Similarities to SAS expressions:

- arithmetic operators
- logical operators (Do not precede AND or OR with %.)
- comparison operators (symbols and mnemonics)
- case sensitivity
- special WHERE operators not valid

Differences compared to SAS expressions:

- Character operands are not quoted.
- Ranges such as 1 <= &x <= 10 behave differently.
- The IN operator does not require parentheses.

7

Special WHERE operators include CONTAINS, IS NULL, IS MISSING, LIKE, BETWEEN-AND, SAME-AND, and =* (sounds like).

Conditional Processing

These *actions* can follow the keywords %THEN and %ELSE:

- a macro language statement
- a macro variable reference
- a macro call
- any text

8

Conditional Processing

The MLOGIC system option displays macro execution messages in the SAS log, including messages about the following:

- macro initialization
- parameter values
- results of arithmetic and logical operations
- macro termination

General form of the MLOGIC|NOMLOGIC option:

OPTIONS MLOGIC;
OPTIONS NOMLOGIC;

The default setting is NOMLOGIC.

9

Macro-Level Programming

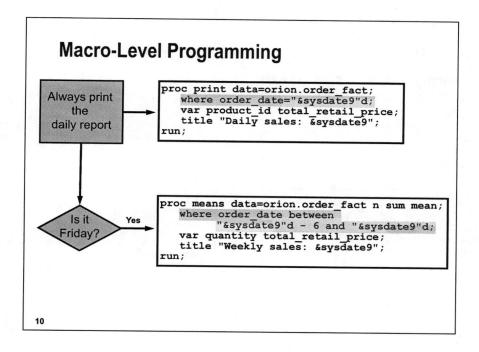

```
proc print data=orion.order_fact;
   where order_date="&sysdate9"d;
   var product_id total_retail_price;
   title "Daily sales: &sysdate9";
run;
```

```
proc means data=orion.order_fact n sum mean;
   where order_date between
        "&sysdate9"d - 6 and "&sysdate9"d;
   var quantity total_retail_price;
   title "Weekly sales: &sysdate9";
run;
```

10

Processing Complete Steps

Method 1: Create separate macros for the **daily** and
           weekly programs.

```
%macro daily;
   proc print data=orion.order_fact;
      where order_date="&sysdate9"d;
      var product_id total_retail_price;
      title "Daily sales: &sysdate9";
   run;
%mend daily;

%macro weekly;
   proc means data=orion.order_fact n sum mean;
      where order_date between
           "&sysdate9"d - 6 and "&sysdate9"d;
      var quantity total_retail_price;
      title "Weekly sales: &sysdate9";
   run;
%mend weekly;
```

m105d01a

11

continued...

Processing Complete Steps

Method 1: Write a third macro that always calls the
DAILY macro and conditionally calls the
WEEKLY macro.

```
%macro reports;
   %daily
   %if &sysday=Friday %then %weekly;
%mend reports;
```

✎ Character constants are not quoted
✎ Character constants are case sensitive.

m105d01a

12

Monitoring Macro Execution

Example: Use the MLOGIC option to monitor the
REPORTS macro.

Partial SAS Log

```
494  %macro reports;
495     %daily
496     %if &sysday=Friday %then %weekly;
497  %mend reports;
498
499  options mlogic;
500  %reports
MLOGIC(REPORTS):  Beginning execution.
MLOGIC(DAILY):  Beginning execution.
MLOGIC(DAILY):  Ending execution.
MLOGIC(REPORTS):  %IF condition &sysday=Friday is TRUE
MLOGIC(WEEKLY):  Beginning execution.
MLOGIC(WEEKLY):  Ending execution.
MLOGIC(REPORTS):  Ending execution.
```

13

✎ The SYMBOLGEN option can be used to debug %IF expressions.

5.01 Quiz

Submit the program **m105a01**. What error do you see in the log?

```
%macro reports;
   %daily
   %if &sysday=Friday then %weekly;
%mend reports;
```

15

Conditional Processing

Use %DO and %END statements following %THEN
or %ELSE to generate text that contains semicolons.

> **%IF** *expression* **%THEN %DO;**
>   *statement*; *statement*;...
> **%END;**
> **%ELSE %DO;**
>   *statement*; *statement*;...
> **%END;**

17

Processing Complete Steps

Method 2: Use a single macro to generate the daily report
unconditionally and the weekly report on Friday.

```
%macro reports;
   proc print data=orion.order_fact;
      where order_date="&sysdate9"d;
      var product_id total_retail_price;
      title "Daily sales: &sysdate9";
   run;
%if &sysday=Friday %then %do;
   proc means data=orion.order_fact n sum mean;
      where order_date between
            "&sysdate9"d - 6 and "&sysdate9"d;
      var quantity total_retail_price;
      title "Weekly sales: &sysdate9";
   run;
%end;
%mend reports;
```

18   m105d01b

Processing Complete Statements

Method 3: Store the production SAS programs in external
files. Copy those files to the input stack with
%INCLUDE statements.

```
%macro reports;
   %include 's:\workshop\daily.sas';
   %if &sysday=Friday %then %do;
       %include 's:\workshop\weekly.sas';
   %end;
%mend reports;
```

m105d01c

The %INCLUDE Statement

The %INCLUDE statement retrieves SAS source code from an external file and places it on the input stack.

General form of the %INCLUDE statement:

> **%INCLUDE** *file-specification* < / SOURCE2 >;

file-specification   is the physical name or fileref of the file to be retrieved and placed on the input stack.

SOURCE2   requests inserted SAS statements to appear in the SAS log.

20

The %INCLUDE Statement

The %INCLUDE statement
- copies SAS statements from an external file to the input stack
- is a global SAS statement
- is not a macro language statement
- can be used only on a statement boundary.

21

Processing Complete Statements

Example: Insert individual statements within a PROC step.

```
%macro count(type=,start=01jan2007,stop=31dec2007);
   proc freq data=orion.order_fact;
      where order_date between "&start"d and "&stop"d;
      table quantity;
      title1 "Orders from &start to &stop";
      %if &type=   %then %do;
         title2 "For All Order Types";
      %end;
      %else %do;
         title2 "For Order Type &type Only";
         where same and order_type=&type;
      %end;
   run;
%mend count;
options mprint mlogic;
%count()
%count(type=3)
```

22   m105d02

Processing Complete Statements

SAS Log

```
802  %count()
MLOGIC(COUNT):  Beginning execution.
MLOGIC(COUNT):  Parameter TYPE has value
MLOGIC(COUNT):  Parameter START has value 01jan2007
MLOGIC(COUNT):  Parameter STOP has value 31dec2007
MPRINT(COUNT):   proc freq data=orion.order_fact;
MPRINT(COUNT):   where order_date between '01jan2007'd and '31dec2007'd;
MPRINT(COUNT):   table quantity;
MPRINT(COUNT):   title1 "Orders from 01jan2007 to 31dec2007";
MLOGIC(COUNT):  %IF condition &type= is TRUE
MPRINT(COUNT):   title2 "For All Order Types";
MPRINT(COUNT):   run;

NOTE: There were 148 observations read from the data set ORION.ORDER_FACT.
      WHERE (order_date>='01JAN2007'D and order_date<='31DEC2007'D);
NOTE: PROCEDURE FREQ used (Total process time):
      real time          0.03 seconds
      cpu time           0.03 seconds

MLOGIC(COUNT):  Ending execution.
```

23

Processing Complete Statements

SAS Log

```
803  %count(type=3)
MLOGIC(COUNT):  Beginning execution.
MLOGIC(COUNT):  Parameter TYPE has value 3
MLOGIC(COUNT):  Parameter START has value 01jan2007
MLOGIC(COUNT):  Parameter STOP has value 31dec2007
MPRINT(COUNT):    proc freq data=orion.order_fact;
MPRINT(COUNT):    where order_date between "01jan2007"d and "31dec2007"d;
MPRINT(COUNT):    table quantity;
MPRINT(COUNT):    title1 "Orders from 01jan2007 to 31dec2007";
MLOGIC(COUNT):  %IF condition &type= is FALSE
MPRINT(COUNT):    title2 "For Order Type 3 only";
MPRINT(COUNT):    where same and order_type=3;
NOTE: Where clause has been augmented.
MPRINT(COUNT):    run;

NOTE: There were 40 observations read from the data set ORION.ORDER_FACT.
      WHERE (order_date>='01JAN2007'D and order_date<='31DEC2007'D) and
      (order_type=3);
NOTE: PROCEDURE FREQ used (Total process time):
      real time            0.01 seconds
      cpu time             0.01 seconds

MLOGIC(COUNT):  Ending execution.
```

24

Processing Complete Statements

Example: Insert individual statements within a DATA step.

```
%macro cust(place);
  %let place=%upcase(&place);
  data customers;
    set orion.customer;
    %if &place=US %then %do;
        where country='US';
        keep customer_name customer_address country;
    %end;
    %else %do;
        where country ne 'US';
        keep customer_name customer_address country location;
        length location $ 12;
        if        country="AU" then location='Australia';
        else if country="CA" then location='Canada';
        else if country="DE" then location='Germany';
        else if country="IL" then location='Israel';
        else if country="TR" then location='Turkey';
        else if country="ZA" then location='South Africa';
    %end;
  run;
%mend cust;
%cust(us)
%cust(international)
```

25   m105d03

The %UPCASE function converts values to uppercase.

%UPCASE(*argument*)

Because macro comparisons are case sensitive, %UPCASE can eliminate case sensitivity when a macro program checks a parameter value.

Processing Complete Statements

SAS Log

```
828  %cust(us)
MLOGIC(CUST):  Beginning execution.
MLOGIC(CUST):  Parameter PLACE has value us
MLOGIC(CUST):  %LET (variable name is PLACE)
MPRINT(CUST):   data customers;
MPRINT(CUST):   set orion.customer;
MLOGIC(CUST):  %IF condition &place=US is TRUE
MPRINT(CUST):   where country='US';
MPRINT(CUST):   keep customer_name customer_address country;
MPRINT(CUST):   run;

NOTE: There were 28 observations read from the data set ORION.CUSTOMER.
      WHERE country='US';
NOTE: The data set WORK.CUSTOMERS has 28 observations and 3 variables.
NOTE: DATA statement used (Total process time):
      real time            0.01 seconds
      cpu time             0.01 seconds

MLOGIC(CUST):  Ending execution.
```

26

Processing Complete Statements

SAS Log

```
829  %cust(international)
MLOGIC(CUST):  Beginning execution.
MLOGIC(CUST):  Parameter PLACE has value international
MLOGIC(CUST):  %LET (variable name is PLACE)
MPRINT(CUST):   data customers;
MPRINT(CUST):   set orion.customer;
MLOGIC(CUST):  %IF condition &place=US is FALSE
MPRINT(CUST):   where country ne 'US';
MPRINT(CUST):   keep customer_name customer_address country location;
MPRINT(CUST):   length location $ 12;
MPRINT(CUST):   if country="AU" then location='Australia';
MPRINT(CUST):   else if country="CA" then location='Canada';
MPRINT(CUST):   else if country="DE" then location='Germany';
MPRINT(CUST):   else if country="IL" then location='Israel';
MPRINT(CUST):   else if country="TR" then location='Turkey';
MPRINT(CUST):   else if country="ZA" then location='South Africa';
MPRINT(CUST):   run;

NOTE: There were 49 observations read from the data set ORION.CUSTOMER.
      WHERE country not = 'US';
NOTE: The data set WORK.CUSTOMERS has 49 observations and 4 variables.
NOTE: DATA statement used (Total process time):
      real time           0.01 seconds
      cpu time            0.01 seconds

MLOGIC(CUST):  Ending execution.
```

27

5.02 Quiz

What is the difference between macro %IF-%THEN and SAS IF-THEN?

29

Processing Partial Statements

Conditionally insert text into the middle of a statement.

Example: Generate either a one-way or two-way frequency
table, depending on parameter values.

```
%macro counts(rows);
    title 'Customer Counts by Gender';
    proc freq data=orion.customer_dim;
        tables
    %if &rows ne  %then &rows *;
        customer_gender;
    run;
%mend counts;

%counts()
%counts(customer_age_group)
```

31   m105d04

Processing Partial Statements

SAS Log

```
1798  %counts()
MPRINT(COUNTS):    title 'Customer Counts by Gender';
MPRINT(COUNTS):    proc freq data=orion.customer_dim;
MPRINT(COUNTS):    tables customer_gender ;
MPRINT(COUNTS):    run;

NOTE: There were 77 observations read from the data set ORION.CUSTOMER_DIM.
NOTE: PROCEDURE FREQ used (Total process time):
      real time            0.03 seconds
      cpu time             0.03 seconds

1799  %counts(customer_age_group)
MPRINT(COUNTS):    title 'Customer Counts by Gender';
MPRINT(COUNTS):    proc freq data=orion.customer_dim;
MPRINT(COUNTS):    tables customer_age_group * customer_gender ;
MPRINT(COUNTS):    run;

NOTE: There were 77 observations read from the data set ORION.CUSTOMER_DIM.
NOTE: PROCEDURE FREQ used (Total process time):
      real time            0.03 seconds
      cpu time             0.03 seconds
```

32

Exercises

Level 1

1. Conditionally Processing Complete Statements

a. Open the **m105e01** program shown below into the Editor window and submit it.

```
%macro listing(custtype);
    proc print data=orion.customer noobs;
    run;
%mend listing;
%listing(2010)
```

b. Modify the macro to test the CUSTTYPE parameter. If the value is null, insert the following statements into the PROC PRINT step:

```
var Customer_ID Customer_Name Customer_Type_ID;
title "All Customers";
```

If the value is not null, insert the following statements into the PROC PRINT step:

```
where Customer_Type_ID=&custtype;
var Customer_ID Customer_Name;
title "Customer Type: &custtype";
```

c. Resubmit the macro definition and call the macro using a null value and a valid value of CUSTTYPE.

Level 2

2. Macro Debugging

a. Open the **m105e02** program shown below into the Editor window.

```
%macro day;
    %if &sysday=SATURDAY
        %then %put Yes;
        %else %put Sorry;
%mend day;

options nomlogic nosymbolgen ;

%day
```

b. Change SATURDAY to today's value and submit the program.

c. Did the log say Yes? If not, take the following steps, in sequence, until it does.

1) Activate the MLOGIC option, resubmit the program, check the log, and change the day as necessary.

2) Activate the SYMBOLGEN option, resubmit the program, check the log, and change the day as necessary.

Level 3

3. Macro Debugging

a. Open the **m105e03** program shown below into the Editor window.

```
%macro where(state);
    %if &state=OR
        %then %put Oregon;
        %else %put Wherever;
%mend where;

%where(CA)
```

b. Submit the program. Examine the log and correct the error.

5.2 Parameter Validation

Objectives

- Perform parameter validation with the OR operator.
- Perform parameter validation with the IN operator.
- Perform data-driven parameter validation.
- Perform parameter validation with the %INDEX function.

36

Parameter Validation

Example: Validate a parameter value before generating
SAS code that is based on that value.

```
%macro customers(place);
   %let place=%upcase(&place);
   %if &place=AU
   or  &place=CA
   or  &place=DE
   or  &place=IL
   or  &place=TR
   or  &place=US
   or  &place=ZA %then %do;
      proc print data=orion.customer;
         var customer_name customer_address country;
         where upcase(country)="&place";
         title "Customers from &place";
      run;
   %end;
   %else %put Sorry, no customers from &place..;
%mend customers;
%customers(de)
%customers(aa)
```

37   m105d05a

5.03 Quiz

Instead of using multiple OR operators, what operator can
you use in the DATA step to determine whether a variable
value is in a list?

```
%macro customers(place);
   %let place=%upcase(&place);
   %if &place=AU
   or  &place=CA
   or  &place=DE
   or  &place=IL
   or  &place=TR
   or  &place=US
   or  &place=ZA %then %do;
      proc print data=orion.customer;
         var customer_name customer_address country;
         where upcase(country)="&place";
         title "Customers from &place";
      run;
   %end;
   %else %put Sorry, no customers from &place..;
%mend customers;
```

39

Parameter Validation

Example: Use the IN operator for parameter validation.

```
%macro customers(place) / minoperator;
   %let place=%upcase(&place);
   %if &place in AU CA DE IL TR US ZA %then %do;
      proc print data=orion.customer;
         var customer_name customer_address country;
         where upcase(country)="&place";
         title "Customers from &place";
      run;
   %end;
   %else %put Sorry, no customers from &place..;
%mend customers;

%customers(de)
%customers(aa)
```

m105d05b

41

The macro IN operator is available in SAS 9.2. The value list is not parenthesized. The MINOPERATOR option is required.

When using NOT with the IN operator, NOT must precede the IN expression. Parentheses are required, as shown below.

```
%if not(&macvar in &valuelist) %then … ;
```

Parameter Validation

SAS Log

```
955  %customers(de)
NOTE: There were 10 observations read from the data set ORION.CUSTOMER.
      WHERE UPCASE(country)='DE';
NOTE: PROCEDURE PRINT used (Total process time):
      real time           0.01 seconds
      cpu time            0.01 seconds

956  %customers(aa)
Sorry, no customers from AA.
```

42

5.04 Quiz

Open program **m105d05c**. How is the macro variable
LIST assigned its value?

```
%macro customers(place) / minoperator;
   %let place=%upcase(&place);
   proc sql noprint;
      select distinct country into :list separated by ' '
             from orion.customer;
   quit;
   %if &place in &list %then %do;
      proc print data=orion.customer;
         var customer_name customer_address country;
         where upcase(country)="&place";
         title "Customers from &place";
      run;
   %end;
   %else %do;
         %put Sorry, no customers from &place..;
         %put Valid countries are: &list..;
   %end;
%mend customers;
```

44

Data-Driven Validation

Example: Use data-driven parameter validation.

```
%macro customers(place) / minoperator;
    %let place=%upcase(&place);
    proc sql noprint;
        select distinct country into :list separated by ' '
            from orion.customer;
    quit;
    %if &place in &list %then %do;
        proc print data=orion.customer;
            var customer_name customer_address country;
            where upcase(country)="&place";
            title "Customers from &place";
        run;
    %end;
    %else %do;
            %put Sorry, no customers from &place..;
            %put Valid countries are: &list..;
    %end;
%mend customers;
```

46   m105d05c

Data-Driven Validation

SAS Log

```
1246  %customers(de)
NOTE: PROCEDURE SQL used (Total process time):
      real time             0.01 seconds
      cpu time              0.01 seconds

NOTE: There were 10 observations read from the data set ORION.CUSTOMER.
      WHERE UPCASE(country)='DE';
NOTE: PROCEDURE PRINT used (Total process time):
      real time             0.00 seconds
      cpu time              0.00 seconds

1247  %customers(a)
NOTE: PROCEDURE SQL used (Total process time):
      real time             0.00 seconds
      cpu time              0.00 seconds

Sorry, no customers from A.
Valid countries are: AU CA DE IL TR US ZA.
```

47

The %INDEX Function (Self-Study)

Use the %INDEX function to check the value of a macro variable against a list of valid values.

General form of the %INDEX function:

> %INDEX(*argument1*, *argument2*)

The %INDEX function does the following:

- searches *argument1* for the first occurrence of *argument2*
- returns an integer representing the position in *argument1* of the first character of *argument2* if there is an exact match
- returns 0 if there is no match

48

The %INDEX Function (Self-Study)

> %INDEX(*argument1*, *argument2*)

argument1 and *argument2* can be the following:

- constant text
- macro variable references
- macro functions
- macro calls

49

Data-Driven Validation (Self-Study)

Example: Use the %INDEX function for parameter validation.

```
%macro customers(place);
   %let place=%upcase(&place);
   proc sql noprint;
      select distinct country into :list separated by '*'
         from orion.customer;
   quit;
   %if %index(*&list*,*&place*) > 0 %then %do;
      proc print data=orion.customer;
          var customer_name customer_address country;
          where upcase(country)="&place";
          title "Customers from &place";
      run;
   %end;
   %else %do;
       %put Sorry, no customers from &place..;
       %put Valid countries are: &list..;
   %end;
%mend customers;
```

50   m105d05d

Extra delimiters are required because the %INDEX function does not consider word boundaries when locating matching text.

Data-Driven Validation (Self-Study)

SAS Log

```
1252  %customers(de)
NOTE: PROCEDURE SQL used (Total process time):
      real time            0.01 seconds
      cpu time             0.01 seconds

NOTE: There were 10 observations read from the data set ORION.CUSTOMER.
      WHERE UPCASE(country)='DE';
NOTE: PROCEDURE PRINT used (Total process time):
      real time            0.00 seconds
      cpu time             0.00 seconds

1253  %customers(a)
NOTE: PROCEDURE SQL used (Total process time):
      real time            0.00 seconds
      cpu time             0.00 seconds

Sorry, no customers from A.
Valid countries are: AU*CA*DE*IL*TR*US*ZA.
```

51

 **Exercises**

Level 1

4. Parameter Validation

a. Open the **m105e04** program shown below into the Editor window and submit it.

```
%macro custtype(type);
   %let type=%upcase(&type);
    proc print data=orion.customer_dim;
       var Customer_Group Customer_Name Customer_Gender
           Customer_Age;
       where upcase(Customer_Group) contains "&type";
       title "&type Customers";
    run;
%mend custtype;
%custtype(internet)
```

b. Modify the macro to use %IF-%THEN and %ELSE statements to validate the TYPE parameter. The macro should submit the PROC PRINT step only if the TYPE parameter is GOLD or INTERNET. If the TYPE parameter is not correct, the macro should write this message to the SAS log:

```
ERROR: Invalid TYPE: xxxx.
ERROR: Valid TYPE values are INTERNET or GOLD.
```

The value *xxxx* is the TYPE parameter.

    Be sure to set the appropriate option to activate the IN operator.

c. Resubmit the macro definition and call the macro using valid and invalid parameter values.

d. Modify the macro to test whether TYPE is null. If so, do not execute PROC PRINT. Instead, the macro should write this message to the SAS log:

```
ERROR: Missing TYPE.
ERROR: Valid values are INTERNET or GOLD.
```

The macro should first check for a null parameter value. If TYPE is not null, the macro should convert TYPE to uppercase and test for valid values of GOLD or INTERNET.

e. Resubmit the macro definition with a null parameter value, valid values in uppercase, lowercase, and mixed case, and an invalid value.

Level 2

5. Data-Driven Parameter Validation

a. Open the **m105e05** program shown below into the Editor window and submit it.

```
%macro listing(custtype);
   %if &custtype= %then %do;
     proc print data=orion.customer noobs;
         var Customer_ID Customer_Name Customer_Type_ID;
         title "All Customers";
     run;
   %end;
   %else %do;
       proc print data=orion.customer noobs;
           where Customer_Type_ID=&custtype;
           var Customer_ID Customer_Name;
           title "Customer Type: &custtype";
       run;
   %end;
%mend listing;


%listing(1020)
%listing()
```

b. Modify the macro definition to validate CUSTTYPE against a data-driven list.

1) Use the SQL procedure to create the macro variable IDLIST that contains the unique values of the variable **Customer_Type_ID** in the **orion.customer_type** data set.

2) If the CUSTTYPE parameter is not missing, validate it against IDLIST.

   ✎   The macro IN operator cannot check for a null value. Check that a value is not null before using the IN operator to check whether the value is valid.

3) If CUSTTYPE is in IDLIST, execute PROC PRINT. Otherwise, do not execute PROC PRINT. Instead, the macro should write this message to the SAS log:

Partial SAS Log

```
ERROR: Value for CUSTTYPE is invalid.
       Valid values are 1010 1020 1030 1040 2010 2020 2030 3010
```

c. Resubmit the macro definition and call the macro with a null parameter value, a valid value, and an invalid value.

Level 3

6. Parameter Validation

a. Open the **m105e06** program shown below into the Editor window and submit it.

```
%macro salarystats(decimals=2,order=internal);
   options nolabel;
   title 'Salary Stats';
   proc means data=orion.staff maxdec=&decimals order=&order;
      where job_title contains 'Sales';
      var salary;
      class job_title;
   run;
title;
%mend salarystats;
```

b. Modify the macro to validate parameters according to the following requirements:

Macro Variable	Possible Values
DECIMALS	0 to 4
ORDER	INTERNAL, FREQ

1) Create an additional macro variable named NUMERRORS that accumulates the number of parameter errors.

2) Execute PROC MEANS only if NUMERRORS is zero.

✎   To express NOT IN, use the syntax below.

%IF NOT(&*macvar* IN &*value-list*) %THEN … ;

c. The macro should write the following messages to the SAS log when parameters are invalid:

Partial SAS Log

```
211  %salarystats(decimals=5,order=fudge)
ERROR: Invalid DECIMALS parameter: 5.
       Valid DECIMALS values are 0 to 4.
ERROR: Invalid ORDER parameter: FUDGE.
       Valid ORDER values are INTERNAL or FREQ.
ERROR: 2 errors.  Code not submitted.
```

5.3 Iterative Processing

Objectives

- Execute macro language statements iteratively.
- Generate SAS code iteratively.

55

Simple Loops

Macro applications might require iterative processing.

The iterative %DO statement can execute macro language statements and generate SAS code.

General form of the iterative %DO statement:

```
%DO index-variable=start %TO stop <%BY increment>;
    text
%END;
```

56

Simple Loops

- %DO and %END statements are valid only inside a macro definition.

- *index-variable* is a macro variable.

- *index-variable* is created in the local symbol table if it does not already exist in another symbol table.

- *start*, *stop*, and *increment* values can be any valid macro expressions that resolve to integers.

- The %BY clause is optional. (The default *increment* is 1.)

57

Simple Loops

text can be any of the following:

- constant text
- macro variables or expressions
- macro statements
- macro calls

58

The SYMPUTX Routine (Review)

Example: Create a numbered series of macro variables.

```
data _null_;
   set orion.country end=no_more;
   call symputx('Country'||left(_n_),country_name);
   if no_more then call symputx('numrows',_n_);
run;
```

SAS Log

```
133  %put _user_;
GLOBAL COUNTRY5 Turkey
GLOBAL COUNTRY2 Canada
GLOBAL COUNTRY3 Germany
GLOBAL COUNTRY1 Australia
GLOBAL NUMROWS 7
GLOBAL COUNTRY6 United States
GLOBAL COUNTRY7 South Africa
GLOBAL COUNTRY4 Israel
```

m105d06

59

The PROC SQL step below creates the same series of macro variables.

```
proc sql noprint;
   select country_name into :country1-:country1000000
      from orion.country;
   %let numrows=&sqlobs;
quit;
```

🖊   The automatic macro variable SQLOBS is populated with the number of rows processed by the SELECT statement.

Simple Loops

Example: Display a series of macro variables in the
SAS log by repeatedly executing %PUT
within a macro loop.

```
%macro putloop;
   %do i=1 %to &numrows;
      %put Country&i is &&country&i;
   %end;
%mend putloop;
```

SAS Log

```
200  %putloop
Country1 is Australia
Country2 is Canada
Country3 is Germany
Country4 is Israel
Country5 is Turkey
Country6 is United States
Country7 is South Africa
```

60   m105d07

No code is sent to the compiler when the macro executes. The %PUT statements are executed by
the macro processor.

Indirect References (Review)

```
%macro putloop;
   %do i=1 %to &numrows;
      %put Country&i is &&country&i;
   %end;
%mend putloop;
```

Partial Symbol Table

Variable	Value
I	1
COUNTRY1	Australia
COUNTRY2	Canada
COUNTRY3	Germany

&&COUNTRY&I ⇨ &COUNTRY1 ⇨ Australia

61

5.05 Multiple Choice Poll

Which statement correctly creates an index variable
named **i**?

a. %do &i=1 %to 10;

b. %do &i=1   to 10;

c. %do i=1 %to 10;

d. %do i=1   to 10;

63

Generating Repetitive Code

Example: Iteratively generate complete SAS steps.

```
%macro readraw(first=2003,last=2007);
   %do year=&first %to &last;
     data year&year;
       infile "s:\workshop\orders&year..dat";
       input order_ID order_type order_date : date9.;
     run;
   %end;
%mend readraw;

options mlogic mprint;

%readraw(first=2004,last=2006)
```

65   m105d08

Generating Repetitive Code

Partial SAS Log

```
MLOGIC(READRAW):   %DO loop index variable YEAR is now 2005; loop will iterate again.
MPRINT(READRAW):   data year2005;
MPRINT(READRAW):   infile "s:\workshop\orders2005.dat";
MPRINT(READRAW):   input order_ID order_type order_date : date9.;
MPRINT(READRAW):   run;

NOTE: The infile "s:\workshop\orders2005.dat" is:
      File Name=s:\workshop\orders2005.dat,
      RECFM=V,LRECL=256

NOTE: 70 records were read from the infile "s:\workshop\orders2005.dat".
      The minimum record length was 22.
      The maximum record length was 22.
NOTE: The data set WORK.YEAR2005 has 70 observations and 3 variables.
NOTE: DATA statement used (Total process time):
      real time           0.01 seconds
      cpu time            0.01 seconds

MLOGIC(READRAW):   %DO loop index variable YEAR is now 2006; loop will iterate again.
MPRINT(READRAW):   data year2006;
MPRINT(READRAW):   infile "s:\workshop\orders2006.dat";
MPRINT(READRAW):   input order_ID order_type order_date : date9.;
MPRINT(READRAW):   run;
```

66

Generating Data-Dependent Code

Example: Create a separate data set for each value
          of a selected variable in a selected data set.

```
%split(data=orion.customer, var=country)
```

Partial SAS Log

```
MPRINT(SPLIT):    data AU CA DE IL TR US ZA ;
MPRINT(SPLIT):    set orion.customer;
MPRINT(SPLIT):    select(country);
MPRINT(SPLIT):    when("AU") output AU;
MPRINT(SPLIT):    when("CA") output CA;
MPRINT(SPLIT):    when("DE") output DE;
MPRINT(SPLIT):    when("IL") output IL;
MPRINT(SPLIT):    when("TR") output TR;
MPRINT(SPLIT):    when("US") output US;
MPRINT(SPLIT):    when("ZA") output ZA;
MPRINT(SPLIT):    otherwise;
MPRINT(SPLIT):    end;
MPRINT(SPLIT):    run;
```

67

Generating Data-Dependent Code

Step 1: Store unique data values into macro variables.

```
%macro split (data=, var=);
  proc sort data=&data(keep=&var) out=values nodupkey;
    by &var;
  run;
  data _null_;
    set values end=last;
    call symputx('site'||left(_n_),&var);
    if last then call symputx('count',_n_);
  run;
  %put _local_;
%mend split;

%split(data=orion.customer, var=country)
```

68   m105d09a

Values of the selected variable must represent valid SAS names. The NOTNAME function detects the position of invalid SAS name characters within a character string.

The statement below writes a macro's local symbol table to the SAS log.

```
%put _local_;
```

Generating Data-Dependent Code

Partial SAS Log

```
SPLIT SITE4 IL
SPLIT DATA orion.customer
SPLIT COUNT 7
SPLIT VAR country
SPLIT SITE3 DE
SPLIT SITE2 CA
SPLIT SITE1 AU
SPLIT SITE7 ZA
SPLIT SITE6 US
SPLIT SITE5 TR
```

69

Generating Data-Dependent Code

Step 2: Use loops to generate the DATA step.

```
%macro split (data=, var=);
  proc sort data=&data(keep=&var) out=values nodupkey;
    by &var;
  run;
  data _null_;
    set values end=last;
    call symputx('site'||left(_n_),&var);
    if last then call symputx('count',_n_);
  run;
  data
    %do i=1 %to &count;
      &&site&i
    %end;
  ;
    set &data;
    select(&var);
    %do i=1 %to &count;
      when("&&site&i") output &&site&i;
    %end;
    otherwise;
    end;
  run;
%mend split;
```

m105d09b

70

Generating Data-Dependent Code

Partial SAS Log

```
MPRINT(SPLIT):    data AU CA DE IL TR US ZA ;
MPRINT(SPLIT):    set orion.customer;
MPRINT(SPLIT):    select(country);
MPRINT(SPLIT):    when("AU") output AU;
MPRINT(SPLIT):    when("CA") output CA;
MPRINT(SPLIT):    when("DE") output DE;
MPRINT(SPLIT):    when("IL") output IL;
MPRINT(SPLIT):    when("TR") output TR;
MPRINT(SPLIT):    when("US") output US;
MPRINT(SPLIT):    when("ZA") output ZA;
MPRINT(SPLIT):    otherwise;
MPRINT(SPLIT):    end;
MPRINT(SPLIT):    run;

NOTE: There were 77 observations read from the data set ORION.CUSTOMER.
NOTE: The data set WORK.AU has 8 observations and 12 variables.
NOTE: The data set WORK.CA has 15 observations and 12 variables.
NOTE: The data set WORK.DE has 10 observations and 12 variables.
NOTE: The data set WORK.IL has 5 observations and 12 variables.
NOTE: The data set WORK.TR has 7 observations and 12 variables.
NOTE: The data set WORK.US has 28 observations and 12 variables.
NOTE: The data set WORK.ZA has 4 observations and 12 variables.
NOTE: DATA statement used (Total process time):
      real time           0.10 seconds
      cpu time            0.10 seconds
```

71

5.06 Quiz

Given the symbol table below, what is the value
of &&SITE&COUNT?

```
SPLIT SITE4 IL
SPLIT DATA orion.customer
SPLIT COUNT 7
SPLIT VAR country
SPLIT SITE3 DE
SPLIT SITE2 CA
SPLIT SITE1 AU
SPLIT SITE7 ZA
SPLIT SITE6 US
SPLIT SITE5 TR
```

73

Generating Data-Dependent Code

SAS metadata is available in the `sashelp.vstabvw`
dynamic view.

```
proc print data=sashelp.vstabvw;
   where libname="ORION";
   title "SASHELP.VSTABVW";
run;
```

Partial PROC PRINT Output

SASHELP.VSTABVW			
Obs	libname	memname	memtype
336	ORION	CITY	DATA
337	ORION	CONTINENT	DATA
338	ORION	COUNTRY	DATA
339	ORION	COUNTY	DATA
340	ORION	CUSTOMER	DATA
341	ORION	CUSTOMER_DIM	DATA

75
m105d10

Generating Data-Dependent Code

Example: Print all data sets in a SAS data library.

Step 1: Store data set names into macro variables.

```
%macro printlib(lib=WORK);
  %let lib=%upcase(&lib);
  data _null_;
    set sashelp.vstabvw end=final;
    where libname="&lib";
    call symputx('dsn'||left(_n_),memname);
    if final then call symputx('totaldsn',_n_);
  run;
  %put _local_;
%mend printlib;

%printlib(lib=orion)
```

m105d11a

76

The statement below writes a macro's local symbol table to the SAS log.

```
%put _local_;
```

Generating Data-Dependent Code

Partial SAS Log

```
PRINTLIB DSN10 ORDER_ITEM
PRINTLIB DSN1 CITY
PRINTLIB DSN11 PRODUCT_DIM
PRINTLIB DSN2 CONTINENT
PRINTLIB DSN12 STAFF
PRINTLIB DSN3 COUNTRY
PRINTLIB DSN13 STATE
PRINTLIB LIB ORION
PRINTLIB DSN4 COUNTY
PRINTLIB DSN5 CUSTOMER
PRINTLIB TOTALDSN 13
PRINTLIB DSN6 CUSTOMER_DIM
PRINTLIB DSN7 EMPLOYEE_PAYROLL
PRINTLIB DSN8 ORDERS
PRINTLIB DSN9 ORDER_FACT
```

77

Generating Data-Dependent Code

Step 2: Use a macro loop to print every data set in the library.

```
%macro printlib(lib=WORK,obs=5);
  %let lib=%upcase(&lib);
  data _null_;
    set sashelp.vstabvw end=final;
    where libname="&lib";
    call symputx('dsn'||left(_n_),memname);
    if final then call symputx('totaldsn',_n_);
  run;
  %do i=1 %to &totaldsn;
    proc print data=&lib..&&dsn&i(obs=&obs);
      title "&lib..&&dsn&i Data Set";
    run;
  %end;
%mend printlib;
%printlib(lib=orion)
```

78   m105d11b

Generating Data-Dependent Code

Partial SAS Log

```
PRINT(PRINTLIB):     proc print data=ORION.CUSTOMER(obs=5);
MPRINT(PRINTLIB):    title "ORION.CUSTOMER Data Set";
MPRINT(PRINTLIB):    run;
NOTE: There were 5 observations read from the data set ORION.CUSTOMER.
NOTE: PROCEDURE PRINT used (Total process time):
      real time            0.00 seconds
      cpu time             0.00 seconds

MPRINT(PRINTLIB):    proc print data=ORION.CUSTOMER_DIM(obs=5);
MPRINT(PRINTLIB):    title "ORION.CUSTOMER_DIM Data Set";
MPRINT(PRINTLIB):    run;
NOTE: There were 5 observations read from the data set ORION.CUSTOMER_DIM.
NOTE: PROCEDURE PRINT used (Total process time):
      real time            0.00 seconds
      cpu time             0.00 seconds

MPRINT(PRINTLIB):    proc print data=ORION.CUSTOMER_TYPE(obs=5);
MPRINT(PRINTLIB):    title "ORION.CUSTOMER_TYPE Data Set";
MPRINT(PRINTLIB):    run;
NOTE: There were 5 observations read from the data set ORION.CUSTOMER_TYPE.
NOTE: PROCEDURE PRINT used (Total process time):
      real time            0.00 seconds
      cpu time             0.00 seconds
```

79

Conditional Iteration (Self-Study)

You can perform conditional iteration in macros with %DO %WHILE and %DO %UNTIL statements.

General form of the %DO %WHILE statement:

```
%DO %WHILE(expression);
    text
%END;
```

A %DO %WHILE loop does the following:
- evaluates *expression* at the top of the loop before the loop executes
- executes repetitively while *expression* is true

80

Conditional Iteration (Self-Study)

General form of the %DO %UNTIL statement:

```
%DO %UNTIL(expression);
    text
%END;
```

expression can be any valid macro expression.

A %DO %UNTIL loop does the following:
- evaluates *expression* at the bottom of the loop after the loop executes
- executes repetitively until *expression* is true
- executes at least once

81

Conditional Iteration (Self-Study)

Example: Generate a conditional number of program
steps, based on a parameter value.

```
%macro stats(datasets);
    %let i=1;
    %let dsn=%scan(&datasets,1);
    %do %while(&dsn ne );
        title "ORION.%upcase(&dsn)";
        proc means data=orion.&dsn n min mean max;
        run;
        %let i=%eval(&i+1);
        %let dsn=%scan(&datasets,&i);
    %end;
%mend stats;

%stats(city state country)
```

82   m105d12a

Conditional Iteration (Self-Study)

SAS Log

```
2243  %stats(city state country)
MPRINT(STATS):    title 'ORION.CITY';
MPRINT(STATS):    proc means data=orion.city n min mean max;
MPRINT(STATS):    run;

NOTE: There were 31 observations read from the data set ORION.CITY.
NOTE: PROCEDURE MEANS used (Total process time):
      real time           0.03 seconds
      cpu time            0.03 seconds

MPRINT(STATS):    title 'ORION.STATE';
MPRINT(STATS):    proc means data=orion.state n min mean max;
MPRINT(STATS):    run;

NOTE: There were 106 observations read from the data set ORION.STATE.
NOTE: PROCEDURE MEANS used (Total process time):
      real time           0.01 seconds
      cpu time            0.01 seconds

MPRINT(STATS):    title 'ORION.COUNTRY';
MPRINT(STATS):    proc means data=orion.country n min mean max;
MPRINT(STATS):    run;

NOTE: There were 7 observations read from the data set ORION.COUNTRY.
NOTE: PROCEDURE MEANS used (Total process time):
      real time           0.01 seconds
      cpu time            0.01 seconds
```

83

Conditional Iteration (Self-Study)

Example: Modify the previous example to validate data
set names.

```
%macro stats(datasets);
   %let i=1;
   %do %until(&dsn= );
      %let dsn=%scan(&datasets,&i);
      %if &dsn= %then %put NOTE: Processing completed.;
      %else %if %sysfunc(exist(orion.&dsn)) %then %do;
         title "ORION.%upcase(&dsn)";
         proc means data=orion.&dsn n min mean max;
            run;
      %end;
      %else %put ERROR: No &dsn dataset in ORION library.;
      %let i=%eval(&i+1);
   %end;
%mend stats;

%stats(discount music orders)
```

84   m105d12b

Conditional Iteration (Self-Study)

SAS Log

```
850  %stats(discount music orders)
MPRINT(STATS):   proc means data=orion.DISCOUNT n min mean max;
MPRINT(STATS):   title "ORION.DISCOUNT";
MPRINT(STATS):   run;

NOTE: There were 697 observations read from the data set ORION.DISCOUNT.
NOTE: PROCEDURE MEANS used (Total process time):
      real time          0.03 seconds
      cpu time           0.03 seconds

ERROR: No MUSIC dataset in ORION library.
MPRINT(STATS):   proc means data=orion.ORDERS n min mean max;
MPRINT(STATS):   title "ORION.ORDERS";
MPRINT(STATS):   run;

NOTE: There were 490 observations read from the data set ORION.ORDERS.
NOTE: PROCEDURE MEANS used (Total process time):
      real time          0.01 seconds
      cpu time           0.01 seconds

NOTE: Processing completed.
```

85

 **Exercises**

Level 1

7. **Macro Loops and Indirect References**

   a. Open the **m105e07** program shown below into the Editor window.

   ```
   proc means data=orion.order_fact sum mean maxdec=2;
      where Order_Type=1;
      var Total_Retail_Price CostPrice_Per_Unit;
      title "Order Type: 1";
   run;
   ```

   b. Define a macro that generates a separate PROC MEANS step for each of the order types in the **orion.order_fact** data set. The values of **Order_Type** are 1, 2, and 3.

   The **orion.lookup_order_type** data set contains the variable **START**, which represents each order type, and the variable **LABEL**, which describes each order type.

   Partial Listing of **orion.lookup_order_type**

START	LABEL
1	Retail Sale
2	Catalog Sale
3	Internet Sale

   c. Modify the following DATA step to create a series of macro variables named TYPE1-TYPE*n*, where *n* is the number of observations in the **orion.lookup_order_type** data set. Each macro variable should receive the value of the data set variable **LABEL**. Place the modified DATA step into the macro definition.

   ```
   data _null_;
      set orion.lookup_order_type;
   run;
   ```

   d. Modify the macro to do the following:
   - create a macro variable ENDLOOP and populate it with the number of observations in the **orion.lookup_order_type** data set
   - use the ENDLOOP macro variable as the stop value for the macro DO loop
   - use an indirect reference to TYPE*x* in the TITLE statement

Level 2

8. Generating Data-Dependent Steps

a. Open the **m105e08** program shown below into the Editor window. This program creates a summary data set named **customer_freq** that summarizes the variable **Total_Retail_Price** by **Customer_ID**, and then sorts by descending **sum**. CALL SYMPUTX creates a series of macro variables named TOP1 through TOP*x*, where *x* is the value of the OBS parameter.

```
%macro tops(obs=3);
    proc means data=orion.order_fact sum nway noprint;
        var Total_Retail_Price;
        class Customer_ID;
        output out=customer_freq sum=sum;
    run;

    proc sort data=customer_freq;
        by descending sum;
    run;

    data _null_;
        set customer_freq(obs=&obs);
        call symputx('top'||left(_n_), Customer_ID);
    run;
%mend tops;

%tops()
%tops(obs=5)
```

b. Modify the macro to print a listing of the top *x* customers from the **orion.customer_dim** data set. Display the variables **Customer_ID**, **Customer_Name**, and **Customer_Type**. Use a macro loop to dynamically generate values for the WHERE statement based on the macro variables TOP1 through TOP*x*.

Partial SAS Log

```
MPRINT(TOPS):    proc print data=orion.customer_dim noobs;
MPRINT(TOPS):    where Customer_ID in ( 16 10 45);
MPRINT(TOPS):    var Customer_ID Customer_Name Customer_Type;
MPRINT(TOPS):    title "Top 3 Customers";
MPRINT(TOPS):    run;
```

```
MPRINT(TOPS):    proc print data=orion.customer_dim noobs;
MPRINT(TOPS):    where Customer_ID in ( 16 10 45 2806 195);
MPRINT(TOPS):    var Customer_ID Customer_Name Customer_Type;
MPRINT(TOPS):    title "Top 5 Customers";
MPRINT(TOPS):    run;
```

Level 3

9. Generating Multiple Macro Calls

   a. Open the **m105e09** program shown below into the Editor window. Submit the program and
   review the result.

```
%macro memberlist(custtype);
   proc print data=Orion.Customer_dim;
      var Customer_Name Customer_ID Customer_Age_Group;
      where Customer_Type="&custtype";
      title "A List of &custtype";
   run;
%mend memberlist;

%macro listall;
   data _null_;
      set orion.customer_type end=final;
      call symputx('type'||left(_n_), Customer_Type);
      if final then call symputx('n',_n_);
   run;
   %put _user_;
%mend listall;

%listall
```

   b. Modify the LISTALL macro to call the MEMBERLIST macro. The result of the macro call
   should create a PROC PRINT step for each customer type. Use a macro loop and indirect
   references to generate the appropriate macro calls.

5.4 Global and Local Symbol Tables

Objectives

- Explain the difference between global and local symbol tables.
- Describe how the macro processor decides which symbol table to use.
- Describe the concept of nested macros and the hierarchy of symbol tables.

89

The Global Symbol Table (Review)

The *global symbol table* is

- created during SAS initialization
- initialized with automatic macro variables
- deleted at the end of the session.

90

The Global Symbol Table

Global macro variables can be created by any of the following:

- %LET statement
- DATA step SYMPUTX routine
- PROC SQL SELECT statement INTO clause
- %GLOBAL statement

91

The %GLOBAL Statement

General form of the %GLOBAL statement:

%GLOBAL *macro-variable1 macro-variable2* . . . ;

- The %GLOBAL statement adds one or more macro variables to the global symbol table with null values.
- It has no effect on variables already in the global table.
- It can be used anywhere in a SAS program.

92

The Local Symbol Table

A *local symbol table* is

- created when a macro with a parameter list is called or a local macro variable is created during macro execution
- deleted when the macro finishes execution.

Macros that do not create local variables do not have a local table.

93

The Local Symbol Table

Local macro variables can be

- created at macro invocation (parameters)
- created during macro execution
- updated during macro execution
- referenced anywhere within the macro.

94

The Local Symbol Table

Use local variables instead of global variables whenever possible. Memory used by a local table can be reused when the table is deleted following macro execution.

Local Symbol Table

Variable	Value
parameter1	value1
parameter2	value2
.	.
.	.
.	.
uservar1	value1
uservar2	value2

95

The Local Symbol Table

Local macro variables can be created by the following **within** a macro definition:

- %LET statement
- DATA step SYMPUTX routine
- PROC SQL SELECT statement INTO clause
- %LOCAL statement

96

The DATA step SYMPUT routine can also create local macro variables.

The %LOCAL Statement

General form of the %LOCAL statement:

> **%LOCAL** *macro-variable1 macro-variable2* . . . ;

- The %LOCAL statement adds one or more macro variables to the local symbol table with null values.
- It has no effect on variables already in the local table.
- It can appear only inside a macro definition.

97

The %LOCAL Statement

Declare the index variable of a macro loop as a local variable to prevent accidental contamination of a like-named macro variable in the global table or another local table.

```
%macro putloop;
   %local i;
   %do i=1 %to &numrows;
      %put Country&i is &&country&i;
   %end;
%mend putloop;
```

98   m105d13

Rules for Creating and Updating Variables

When the macro processor receives a request to create or update a macro variable **during macro execution**, the macro processor follows these rules:

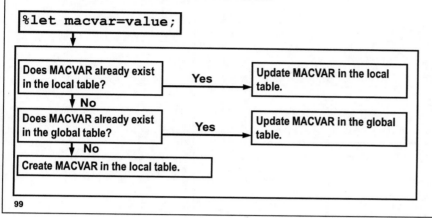

```
%let macvar=value;
```

Does MACVAR already exist in the local table?	Yes →	Update MACVAR in the local table.
No ↓		
Does MACVAR already exist in the global table?	Yes →	Update MACVAR in the global table.
No ↓		
Create MACVAR in the local table.		

99

Rules for Resolving Variables

To resolve a macro variable reference **during macro execution**, the macro processor follows these rules:

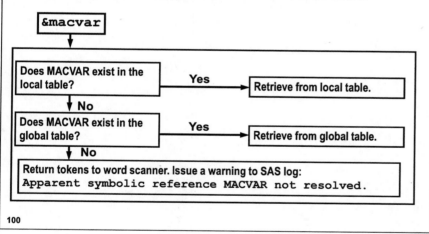

```
&macvar
```

Does MACVAR exist in the local table?	Yes →	Retrieve from local table.
No ↓		
Does MACVAR exist in the global table?	Yes →	Retrieve from global table.
No ↓		
Return tokens to word scanner. Issue a warning to SAS log: `Apparent symbolic reference MACVAR not resolved.`		

100

5.07 Quiz

How many local symbol tables are created when macro A
is called and begins to execute?

```
%macro a(value=);
   %b
%mend a;

%macro b;
     %put The value to write is: &value.;
     %put _user_;
%macro b;

%a(value=Today is Monday)
```

Multiple Local Tables

Multiple local tables can exist concurrently during macro execution.

Example: Define two macros. One calls the other.

```
%macro outer;
    %local x;
    %let x=1;
    %inner
%mend outer;
%macro inner;
    %local y;
    %let y=&x;
%mend inner;
```

104

Multiple Local Tables

Create global macro variable X.

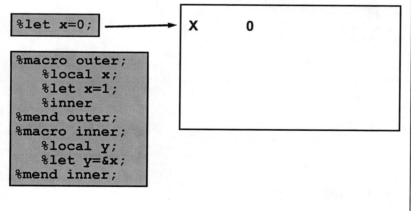

Global Table

```
%let x=0;
```

X	0

```
%macro outer;
    %local x;
    %let x=1;
    %inner
%mend outer;
%macro inner;
    %local y;
    %let y=&x;
%mend inner;
```

105

Multiple Local Tables

Call the OUTER macro. When the %LOCAL statement executes, a local table is created.

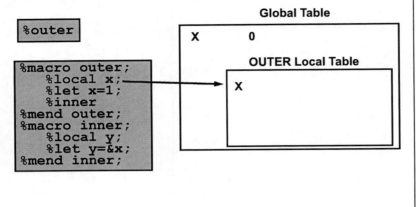

```
%outer
```

Global Table

X   0

OUTER Local Table

X

```
%macro outer;
    %local x;
    %let x=1;
    %inner
%mend outer;
%macro inner;
    %local y;
    %let y=&x;
%mend inner;
```

106

Multiple Local Tables

The %LET statement updates local macro variable X. Access to global macro variable X is blocked.

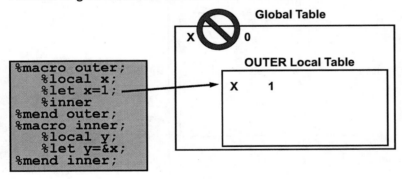

Global Table

X   0

OUTER Local Table

X   1

```
%macro outer;
    %local x;
    %let x=1;
    %inner
%mend outer;
%macro inner;
    %local y;
    %let y=&x;
%mend inner;
```

What happens if the %LOCAL statement in the OUTER

107   macro is omitted?

Multiple Local Tables

A nested macro call can create its own local symbol table in addition to any other tables that might currently exist.

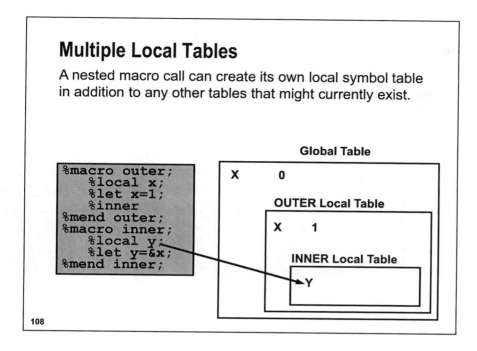

108

Multiple Local Tables

The macro processor resolves a macro variable reference by searching symbol tables in the reverse order in which they were created, as follows:

1. current local table
2. previously created local tables
3. global table

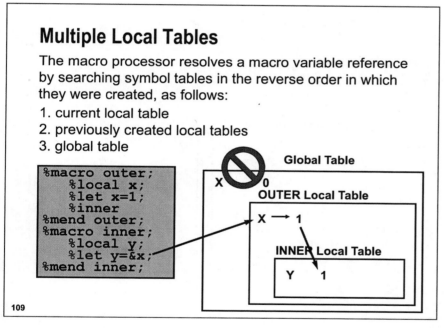

109

The global variable X is **not** available to the INNER macro.

Multiple Local Tables

When the INNER macro finishes execution, its local table is deleted. Control returns to the OUTER macro.

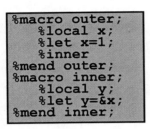

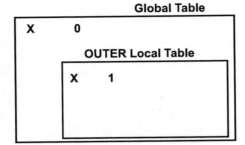

Global Table

X	0

OUTER Local Table

X	1

110

Multiple Local Tables

When the OUTER macro finishes execution, its local table is deleted. Only the GLOBAL table remains.

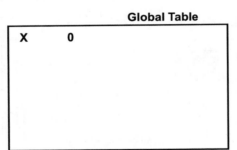

Global Table

X	0

111

The SYMPUTX Routine

The optional *scope* argument of the SYMPUTX routine specifies where to store the macro variable:

CALL SYMPUTX(*macro-variable*, *text* <,*scope*>**);**

- G specifies the global symbol table.
- L specifies the current macro's local symbol table. If no local symbol table exists for the current macro, a local symbol table is created.

112

The *scope* argument is recommended any time the SYMPUTX routine is used within a macro definition.

Multiple Local Tables

Example: The NUMOBS macro returns the number of observations in a SAS data set.

```
%macro numobs(lib,dsn);
   options nonotes;
   data _null_;
      call symputx('num', number,'G');
      stop;
      set &lib..&dsn nobs=number;
   run;
   options notes;
%mend numobs;
```

SAS Log

```
1831   %numobs(orion,order_fact);
1832   %put ---> &num observations;
--->   617 observations
```

113   m105d14

The STOP statement stops DATA step execution. The special variable NUMBER is populated during compile time.

5.08 Quiz

Open and submit program **m105a02**.

Why did you receive a warning message regarding NUM?

```
%macro numobsL(lib,dsn);
   options nonotes;
   data _null_;
      call symputx('num', number);
      stop;
      set &lib..&dsn nobs=number;
   run;
   options notes;
%mend numobsL;

%numobsL(orion,order_fact);
%put --->   &num observations;
```

115

Multiple Local Tables

Example: The CHECK macro calls the NUMOBS macro.

```
%macro check(month=,year=);
data internet;
    keep order_date order_type quantity total_retail_price;
    set orion.order_fact;
    where order_type=3 and month(order_date)=&month
                      and   year(order_date)=&year;
run;
%numobs(work,internet)
%if &num=0 %then %put No internet orders this month.;
%else %do;
    title1 "Internet Orders &month-&year";
    %if &num>10
        %then %do; title2 "First 10 of &Num Orders"; %end;
        %else %do; title2 "All &Num Orders";          %end;
    proc print data=internet(obs=10);
        var order_date quantity total_retail_price;
    run;
%end;
%mend check;
```

117   m105d14

Multiple Local Tables

SAS Log

```
1114  %check(month=11,year=2007)

NOTE: There were 0 observations read from the data set ORION.ORDER_FACT.
      WHERE (order_type=3) and (MONTH(order_date)=11) and
      (YEAR(order_date)=2007);
NOTE: The data set WORK.INTERNET has 0 observations and 4 variables.
NOTE: DATA statement used (Total process time):
      real time          0.01 seconds
      cpu time           0.01 seconds

No internet orders 11-2007.
1115  %check(month=12,year=2007)

NOTE: There were 2 observations read from the data set ORION.ORDER_FACT.
      WHERE (order_type=3) and (MONTH(order_date)=12) and
      (YEAR(order_date)=2007);
NOTE: The data set WORK.INTERNET has 2 observations and 4 variables.
NOTE: DATA statement used (Total process time):
      real time          0.01 seconds
      cpu time           0.01 seconds

NOTE: There were 2 observations read from the data set WORK.INTERNET.
NOTE: PROCEDURE PRINT used (Total process time):
      real time          0.00 seconds
      cpu time           0.00 seconds
```

118

Multiple Local Tables

Call the CHECK macro.

Parameters are added to the CHECK macro's local table.

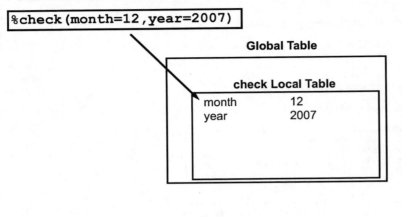

`%check(month=12,year=2007)`

Global Table

check Local Table

month	12
year	2007

119

Multiple Local Tables

The CHECK macro calls the NUMOBS macro.

Parameters are added to the NUMOBS macro's local table.

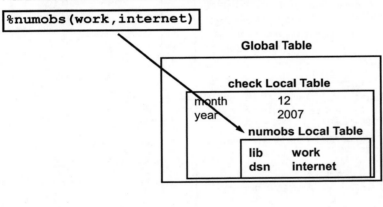

`%numobs(work,internet)`

Global Table

check Local Table

month	12
year	2007

numobs Local Table

lib	work
dsn	internet

120

Multiple Local Tables

The NUMOBS macro begins execution.

```
%macro numobs(lib,dsn);
data _null_;
   call symputx('num',number,'G');
   stop;
   set &lib..&dsn nobs=number;
run;
%mend numobs;
```

Global Table

check Local Table

month	12
year	2007

numobs Local Table

lib	work
dsn	internet

121

Multiple Local Tables

Word scanning begins. DATA step compilation begins.
Macro variable references are encountered.

```
%macro numobs(lib,dsn);
data _null_;
   call symputx('num',number,'G');
   stop;
   set &lib..&dsn nobs=number;
run;
%mend numobs;
```

Global Table

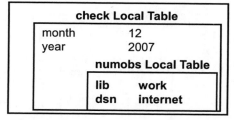

check Local Table

month	12
year	2007

numobs Local Table

lib	work
dsn	internet

122

Multiple Local Tables

Macro variables LIB and DSN resolve.

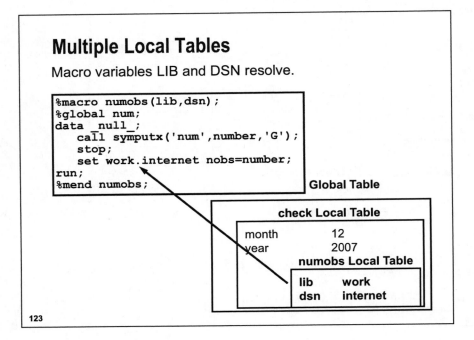

```
%macro numobs(lib,dsn);
%global num;
data _null_;
   call symputx('num',number,'G');
   stop;
   set work.internet nobs=number;
run;
%mend numobs;                          Global Table
```

check Local Table

| month | 12 |
| year | 2007 |

numobs Local Table

| lib | work |
| dsn | internet |

123

Multiple Local Tables

A step boundary is encountered. The SYMPUTX routine
executes. Macro variable NUM is added to the global table.

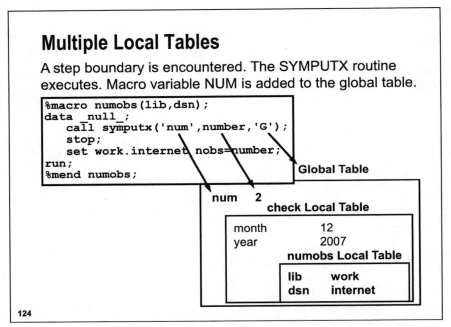

```
%macro numobs(lib,dsn);
data _null_;
   call symputx('num',number,'G');
   stop;
   set work.internet nobs=number;
run;
%mend numobs;                          Global Table
```

num   2

check Local Table

| month | 12 |
| year | 2007 |

numobs Local Table

| lib | work |
| dsn | internet |

124

Multiple Local Tables

The NUMOBS macro finishes execution. Its local symbol table is deleted. Control returns to the CHECK macro.

Global Table

num	2	

check Local Table

month	12
year	2007

125

Multiple Local Tables

The CHECK macro finishes execution. Its local symbol table is deleted. NUM remains in the global table.

Global Table

num	2

126

Exercises

Level 1

10. Understanding Symbol Tables

Without submitting the programs, identify in which symbol table the macro variable DOG is located.

Assume that each example is submitted in a new SAS session.

a.

```
%let dog=Paisley;
%macro whereisit;
    %put My dog is &dog;
%mend whereisit;

%whereisit
```

b.

```
%macro whereisit;
    %let dog=Paisley;
    %put My dog is &dog;
%mend whereisit;

%whereisit
```

c.

```
%macro whereisit(dog);
    %put My dog is &dog;
%mend whereisit;

%whereisit(Paisley)
```

Level 2

11. **Controlling Macro Variable Storage**

   a. Open the **m105e11** program shown below into the Editor window.

```
%macro varscope;
   data _null_;
      set orion.customer_type end=final;
      call symputx('localtype'||left(_n_), Customer_Type);
      if final then call symputx('localn',_n_);
   run;
   %put _user_;
%mend varscope;

%varscope
```

   b. Modify the program so that all macro variables that are created in the DATA step are stored in the **local** symbol table.

   c. Modify the program by adding the following statement before the DATA step and removing the scope specification in the SYMPUTX routine:

```
%local x;
```

   In which symbol table are the macro variables stored?

   d. Modify the program so that all macro variables that are created in the DATA step are stored in the **global** symbol table.

Level 3

12. Creating Multiple Symbol Tables

a. Open the **cleanup** program and submit the macro to delete all global macro variables.

b. Open the **m105e12** program shown below into the Editor window.

```
%macro createmacvar;
   data _null_;
      set orion.lookup_order_type end=last;
      call symputx('type'||left(start), label,'L');
      if last then call symputx('endloop', _n_,'L');
   run;
%mend createmacvar;

%macro sumreport;
   %createmacvar
   %do num=1 %to &endloop;
      proc means data=orion.order_fact sum mean maxdec=2;
         where Order_Type = &num;
         var Total_Retail_Price CostPrice_Per_Unit;
         title "Summary Report for &&type&num";
      run;
   %end;
%mend sumreport;

%sumreport
```

Submit the program. Review and describe the results.

_____

_____

_____

c. Correct the program so that the SUMREPORT macro executes correctly and does not create any global macro variables. Verify that the title resolves properly. In addition, add an **s** to the end of the type description in the title.

PROC MEANS Output

```
                      Summary Report for Retail Sales

                         The MEANS Procedure
 Variable              Label                                 Sum          Mean

 Total_Retail_Price    Total Retail Price for This Product   44654.56    137.82
 CostPrice_Per_Unit    Cost Price Per Unit                   11730.73     36.21
```

```
                      Summary Report for Catalog Sales

                         The MEANS Procedure

 Variable              Label                                 Sum          Mean

 Total_Retail_Price    Total Retail Price for This Product   33931.35    199.60
 CostPrice_Per_Unit    Cost Price Per Unit                    8718.45     51.29
```

```
                      Summary Report for Internet Sales

                         The MEANS Procedure
 Variable              Label                                 Sum          Mean

 Total_Retail_Price    Total Retail Price for This Product   21491.55    174.73
 CostPrice_Per_Unit    Cost Price Per Unit                    5356.95     43.55
```

5.5 Chapter Review

Chapter Review

1. What macro language statements perform conditional processing?

2. Which option causes the SAS log to display the results of arithmetic and logical operations?

3. When is the global symbol table created?

4. When is the global symbol table deleted?

129

Chapter Review

5. Which statement adds several macro variables with null values to the global symbol table?

6. Where can a %LOCAL statement be used?

7. When is a local symbol table created?

8. When is a local symbol table deleted?

131

5.6 Solutions

Solutions to Exercises

1. **Conditionally Processing Complete Statements**

   a. Open the program into the Editor window.

   b. Modify the macro to test the CUSTTYPE parameter. If the value is null, insert VAR and TITLE statements into the PROC PRINT step. If the value is not null, insert WHERE, VAR, and TITLE statements into the PROC PRINT step.

   ```
   %macro listing(custtype);
       proc print data=orion.customer noobs;
       %if &custtype= %then %do;
           var Customer_ID Customer_Name Customer_Type_ID;
           title "All Customers";
       %end;
       %else %do;
           where Customer_Type_ID=&custtype;
           var Customer_ID Customer_Name;
           title "Customer Type: &custtype";
       %end;
       run;
   %mend listing;
   ```

   c. Resubmit the macro definition using a null value and a valid value for CUSTTYPE.

   Partial SAS Log

   ```
   36   %listing()
   MPRINT(LISTING):    proc print data=orion.customer noobs;
   MPRINT(LISTING):    var Customer_ID Customer_Name Customer_Type_ID;
   MPRINT(LISTING):    title "All Customers";
   MPRINT(LISTING):    run;

   NOTE: There were 77 observations read from the data set ORION.CUSTOMER.
   NOTE: PROCEDURE PRINT used (Total process time):
         real time           0.23 seconds
         cpu time            0.01 seconds

   37   %listing(2010)
   MPRINT(LISTING):    proc print data= orion.customer noobs;
   MPRINT(LISTING):    where Customer_Type_ID=2010;
   MPRINT(LISTING):    var Customer_ID Customer_Name;
   MPRINT(LISTING):    title "Customer Type: 2010";
   MPRINT(LISTING):    run;

   NOTE: There were 5 observations read from the data set ORION.CUSTOMER.
         WHERE Customer_Type_ID=2010;
   NOTE: PROCEDURE PRINT used (Total process time):
         real time           1.13 seconds
         cpu time            0.01 seconds
   ```

2. Macro Debugging

a. Open the program into the Editor window.

b. Change SATURDAY to today's value and submit the program.

c. Change today's value to the day you launched SAS. Type the day in mixed case – for example, Tuesday.

3. Macro Debugging

a. Open the program into the Editor window.

b. The %STR function is required to interpret OR as plain text instead of a logical operator.

```
%macro where(state);
   %if &state=%str(OR)
      %then %put Oregon;
      %else %put Wherever;
%mend where;
```

4. Parameter Validation

a. Open the program into the Editor window and submit it.

b. Use %IF to validate the TYPE parameter. The MINOPERATOR option in the %MACRO statement activates the IN operator.

```
%macro custtype(type)/minoperator;
   %let type=%upcase(&type);
   %if &type in GOLD INTERNET %then %do;
      proc print data=orion.customer_dim;
         var Customer_Group Customer_Name Customer_Gender
            Customer_Age;
         where upcase(Customer_Group) contains "&type";
         title "&type Customers";
      run;
   %end;
   %else %do;
      %put ERROR: Invalid TYPE: &type..;
      %put ERROR: Valid TYPE values are INTERNET or GOLD.;
   %end;
%mend custtype;
```

c. Resubmit the macro definition and call the macro using valid and invalid parameter values.

Partial SAS Log

```
248  %custtype(internet)

NOTE: There were 8 observations read from the data set ORION.CUSTOMER_DIM.
      WHERE UPCASE(Customer_Group) contains 'INTERNET';
NOTE: PROCEDURE PRINT used (Total process time):
      real time           0.00 seconds
      cpu time            0.00 seconds

249  %custtype(silver)
ERROR: Invalid TYPE: SILVER.
```

d. Modify the macro to test whether TYPE is null. If so, do not execute PROC PRINT. Instead, the macro should write messages to the SAS log.

```
%macro custtype(type)/minoperator;
   %if &type= %then %do;
      %put ERROR: Missing TYPE.;
      %put ERROR: Valid TYPE values are INTERNET or GOLD.;
   %end;
   %else %do;
      %let type=%upcase(&type);
      %if &type in GOLD INTERNET %then %do;
         proc print data=orion.customer_dim;
            var Customer_Group Customer_Name Customer_Gender
               Customer_Age;
            where upcase(Customer_Group) contains "&type";
            title "&type Customers";
         run;
      %end;
      %else %do;
         %put ERROR: Invalid TYPE: &type..;
         %put ERROR: Valid TYPE values are INTERNET or GOLD.;
      %end;
   %end;
%mend custtype;
```

e. Resubmit the macro definition with a null parameter value, a valid value, and an invalid value.

Partial SAS Log

```
272  %custtype()
ERROR: Missing TYPE.
ERROR: Valid TYPE values are INTERNET or GOLD.
273  %custtype(internet)

NOTE: There were 8 observations read from the data set ORION.CUSTOMER_DIM.
      WHERE UPCASE(Customer_Group) contains 'INTERNET';
NOTE: PROCEDURE PRINT used (Total process time):
      real time           0.00 seconds
      cpu time            0.00 seconds


274  %custtype(silver)
ERROR: Invalid TYPE: SILVER.
ERROR: Valid TYPE values are INTERNET or GOLD.
```

5. Data-Driven Parameter Validation

a. Open the program into the Editor window and submit it.

b. Modify the macro definition to validate CUSTTYPE against a data-driven list.

   1) Use the SQL procedure to create the macro variable IDLIST that contains the unique values of the variable **Customer_Type_ID** in the **orion.customer_type** data set.

   2) Validate the CUSTTYPE parameter against IDLIST.

   3) If CUSTTYPE is in IDLIST, execute PROC PRINT. Otherwise, do not execute PROC PRINT. Instead, the macro should write this message to the SAS log:

Partial SAS Log

```
ERROR: Invalid CUSTTYPE.
       Valid CUSTTYPEs: 1010 1020 1030 1040 2010 2020 2030 3010.
```

```
%macro listing(custtype) / minoperator;
   %if &custtype=  %then %do;
      proc print data= orion.customer noobs;
         var Customer_ID Customer_Name Customer_Type_ID;
         title "All Customers";
      run;
   %end;
   %else %do;
      proc sql noprint;
         select distinct Customer_Type_ID
            into :IDlist separated by ' '
            from orion.customer_type;
      quit;
      %if &custtype in &idlist %then %do;
         proc print data= orion.customer noobs;
            where Customer_Type_ID =&custtype;
            var Customer_ID Customer_Name;
            title "Customer Type: &custtype";
         run;
      %end;
      %else %do;
         %put ERROR: Invalid CUSTTYPE.;
         %put ERROR- Valid CUSTTYPEs: &IDlist..;
      %end;
   %end;
%mend listing;
```

c. Resubmit the macro definition and call the macro with a null parameter value, a valid value, and an invalid value.

Partial SAS Log

```
411  %listing()
MPRINT(LISTING):    proc print data= orion.customer noobs;
MPRINT(LISTING):    var Customer_ID Customer_Name Customer_Type_ID;
MPRINT(LISTING):    title "All Customers";
MPRINT(LISTING):    run;

NOTE: There were 77 observations read from the data set ORION.CUSTOMER.
NOTE: PROCEDURE PRINT used (Total process time):
      real time            0.01 seconds
      cpu time             0.01 seconds

412  %listing(1020)
MPRINT(LISTING):    proc sql noprint;
MPRINT(LISTING):    select distinct Customer_Type_ID into :IDlist separated by ' ' from
orion.customer_type;
MPRINT(LISTING):    quit;
NOTE: PROCEDURE SQL used (Total process time):
      real time            0.00 seconds
      cpu time             0.00 seconds

MPRINT(LISTING):    proc print data= orion.customer noobs;
MPRINT(LISTING):    where Customer_Type_ID =1020;
MPRINT(LISTING):    var Customer_ID Customer_Name;
MPRINT(LISTING):    title "Customer Type: 1020";
MPRINT(LISTING):    run;
NOTE: There were 17 observations read from the data set ORION.CUSTOMER.
      WHERE Customer_Type_ID=1020;
NOTE: PROCEDURE PRINT used (Total process time):
      real time            0.00 seconds
      cpu time             0.00 seconds

413  %listing(9999)
MPRINT(LISTING):    proc sql noprint;
MPRINT(LISTING):    select distinct Customer_Type_ID into :IDlist separated by ' ' from
orion.customer_type;
MPRINT(LISTING):    quit;
NOTE: PROCEDURE SQL used (Total process time):
      real time            0.00 seconds
      cpu time             0.00 seconds

ERROR: Invalid CUSTTYPE.
       Valid CUSTTYPEs: 1010 1020 1030 1040 2010 2020 2030 3010.
```

6. Parameter Validation

a. Open the program into the Editor window and submit it.

b. Modify the macro to validate parameters according to the following requirements:

Macro Variable	Possible Values
DECIMALS	0 to 4
ORDER	INTERNAL, FREQ

1) Create an additional macro variable named NUMERRORS that accumulates the number of parameter errors.

2) Execute PROC MEANS only if NUMERRORS is zero.

The macro should write messages to the SAS log when parameters are invalid.

```
%macro salarystats(decimals=2,order=internal)/minoperator;
   %let numerrors=0;
   %if not (&decimals in 0 1 2 3 4) %then %do;
      %let numerrors=%eval(&numerrors+1);
      %put ERROR: Invalid DECIMALS parameter: &decimals..;
      %put ERROR- Valid DECIMALS values are 0 to 4.;
   %end;
   %let order=%upcase(&order);
   %if not (&order in INTERNAL FREQ) %then %do;
      %let numerrors=%eval(&numerrors+1);
      %put ERROR: Invalid ORDER parameter: &order..;
      %put ERROR- Valid ORDER values are INTERNAL or FREQ.;
   %end;
   %if &numerrors=0 %then %do;
     options nolabel;
     title 'Salary Stats';
     proc means data=orion.staff maxdec=&decimals order=&order;
        where job_title contains 'Sales';
        var salary;
        class job_title;
     run;
     title;
   %end;
   %else %put ERROR: &numerrors errors. Code not submitted.;
%mend salarystats;

%salarystats()
%salarystats(decimals=5,order=fudge)
```

7. Macro Loops and Indirect References

a. Open the program into the Editor window.

b. Define a macro that generates a separate PROC MEANS step for each of the order types in the **orion.order_fact** data set. The values of **Order_Type** are 1, 2, and 3.

```
%macro sumreport;
   %do num=1 %to 3;
      proc means data=orion.order_fact sum mean maxdec=2;
         where Order_Type=&num;
         var Total_Retail_Price CostPrice_Per_Unit;
         title "Order Type: &num";
      run;
   %end;
%mend sumreport;

%sumreport
```

c. Insert the provided DATA step to create the series of macro variables.

d. Modify the macro to use the following:

- the ENDLOOP macro variable as the stop value for the iterative DO loop

- an indirect reference to TYPE*x* in the TITLE statement

```
%macro sumreport;
   data _null_;
      set orion.lookup_order_type end=last;
      call symputx('type'||left(_n_), label);
      if last then call symputx('endloop', _n_);
   run;
   %do num=1 %to &endloop;
      proc means data=orion.order_fact sum mean maxdec=2;
         where Order_Type=&num;
         var Total_Retail_Price CostPrice_Per_Unit;
         title "Order Type: &&type&num";
      run;
   %end;
%mend sumreport;

%sumreport
```

8. Generating Data-Dependent Steps

a. Open the program into the Editor window.

b. Modify the macro to print a listing of the top *x* customers from the **orion.customer_dim** data set. Display the variables **Customer_ID**, **Customer_Name**, and **Customer_Type**. Use a macro loop to dynamically generate values for the WHERE statement based on the macro variables TOP1 through TOP*x*.

```
%macro tops(obs=3);
   proc means data=orion.order_fact sum nway noprint;
      var Total_Retail_Price;
      class Customer_ID;
      output out=customer_freq sum=sum;
   run;

   proc sort data=customer_freq;
      by descending sum;
   run;

   data _null_;
      set customer_freq(obs=&obs);
      call symputx('top'||left(_n_), Customer_ID);
   run;

   proc print data=orion.customer_dim noobs;
      where Customer_ID in (%do num=1 %to &obs; &&top&num %end;);
      var Customer_ID Customer_Name Customer_Type;
      title "Top &obs Customers";
   run;
%mend tops;

%tops()
%tops(obs=5)
```

9. Generating Multiple Macro Calls

a. Review the output generated by the LISTALL macro in program **m105e09**.

```
GLOBAL TYPE8 Internet/Catalog Customers
GLOBAL TYPE4 Orion  Club members high activity
GLOBAL TYPE5 Orion Club Gold members low activity
GLOBAL TYPE6 Orion Club Gold members medium activity
GLOBAL TYPE7 Orion Club Gold members high activity
GLOBAL N 8
GLOBAL TYPE1 Orion Club members inactive
GLOBAL TYPE2 Orion Club members low activity
GLOBAL TYPE3 Orion  Club members medium activity
```

b. Modify the LISTALL macro to call the MEMBERLIST macro. The result of the macro call should create a PROC PRINT step for each customer type. Use a macro loop and indirect references to generate the appropriate macro calls.

```
%macro memberlist(custtype);
   proc print data=Orion.Customer_dim;
      var Customer_Name Customer_ID Customer_Age_Group;
      where Customer_Type="&custtype";
      title "A List of &custtype";
   run;
%mend memberlist;

%macro listall;
   data _null_;
      set orion.customer_type end=final;
      call symputx('type'||left(_n_), Customer_Type);
      if final then call symputx('n',_n_);
   run;
   %do num=1 %to &n;
      %memberlist(&&type&num)
   %end;
%mend listall;

%listall
```

10. **Understanding Symbol Tables**

Without submitting the programs, identify in which symbol table the macro variable DOG is located.

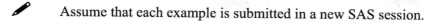 Assume that each example is submitted in a new SAS session.

a. Because the %LET statement is outside the macro definition, the macro variable DOG is stored in the global symbol table.

```
%let dog=Paisley;
%macro whereisit;
   %put My dog is &dog;
%mend whereisit;
%whereisit
```

b. Because the %LET statement is inside the macro definition, the macro variable DOG is stored in the local symbol table.

```
%macro whereisit;
   %let dog=Paisley;
   %put My dog is &dog;
%mend whereisit;
%whereisit
```

c. Because DOG is a macro parameter, it is stored in the local symbol table.

```
%macro whereisit(dog);
   %put My dog is &dog;
%mend whereisit;
%whereisit(Paisley)
```

11. Controlling Macro Variable Storage

a. Open the program into the Editor window.

b. Specifying **L** as the third argument of the SYMPUTX routine stores the macro variable in the local symbol table.

```
%macro varscope;
   data _null_;
      set orion.customer_type end=final;
      call symputx('localtype'||left(_n_), Customer_Type,'L');
      if final then call symputx('localn',_n_,'L');
   run;
   %put _user_;
%mend varscope;
%varscope
```

c. By adding the %LOCAL statement and removing the scope specification, the SYMPUTX routine creates local macro variables.

```
2     %macro varscope;
3        %local x;
4        data _null_;
5           set orion.customer_type end=final;
6           call symputx('localtype'||left(_n_), Customer_Type);
7           if final then call symputx('localn',_n_);
8        run;
9        %put _user_;
10    %mend varscope;
11
12    %varscope

NOTE: Numeric values have been converted to character values at the places given by:
      (Line):(Column).
      1:94
NOTE: There were 8 observations read from the data set ORION.CUSTOMER_TYPE.
NOTE: DATA statement used (Total process time):
      real time           0.01 seconds
      cpu time            0.01 seconds


VARSCOPE X
VARSCOPE LOCALTYPE1 Orion Club members inactive
VARSCOPE LOCALTYPE2 Orion Club members low activity
VARSCOPE LOCALTYPE3 Orion  Club members medium activity
VARSCOPE LOCALTYPE4 Orion  Club members high activity
VARSCOPE LOCALTYPE5 Orion Club Gold members low activity
VARSCOPE LOCALTYPE6 Orion Club Gold members medium activity
VARSCOPE LOCALTYPE7 Orion Club Gold members high activity
VARSCOPE LOCALTYPE8 Internet/Catalog Customers
VARSCOPE LOCALN 8
```

d. Specifying **G** as the third argument of the SYMPUTX routine stores the macro variables in the global symbol table.

```
%macro varscope;
   %local x;
   data _null_;
      set orion.customer_type end=final;
      call symputx('localtype'||left(_n_), Customer_Type,'G');
      if final then call symputx('localn',_n_,'G');
   run;
   %put _user_;
%mend varscope;
%varscope
```

12. **Creating Multiple Symbol Tables**

a. Open the **cleanup** program and submit the macro.

b. The macro variables ENDLOOP and TYPE*x* are stored in the local symbol table for the CREATEMACVAR macro and are not available to the SUMREPORT macro. Delete the scope argument from the SYMPUTX routine and add the %LOCAL statement to the SUMREPORT macro to force the macro variables into the local symbol table for the SUMREPORT macro.

c. Correct the program so that the SUMREPORT macro executes correctly and does not create any global macro variables. Verify that the title resolves properly. In addition, add an **s** to the end of the type description in the title.

```
%macro createmacvar;
   data _null_;
      set orion.lookup_order_type end=last;
      call symputx('type'||left(start), label);
      if last then call symputx('endloop', _n_);
   run;
%mend createmacvar;

%macro sumreport;
   %createmacvar
   %do num=1 %to &endloop;
      proc means data=orion.order_fact sum mean maxdec=2;
         where Order_Type = &num;
         var Total_Retail_Price CostPrice_Per_Unit;
         title "Summary Report for &&type&num..s";
      run;
   %end;
%mend sumreport;
%sumreport
```

Solutions to Student Activities (Polls/Quizzes)

5.01 Quiz – Correct Answer

Submit the program **m105a01**. What error do you see in the log?

Partial SAS Log

```
514  %macro reports;
515     %daily
516     %if &sysday=Friday then %weekly;
ERROR: Expected %THEN statement not found.  A dummy macro will be
       compiled.
517  %mend reports;
```

If a macro definition contains macro language syntax errors, error messages are written to the SAS log and a dummy (nonexecutable) macro is created.

16

5.02 Quiz – Correct Answer

What is the difference between macro %IF-%THEN and SAS IF-THEN?

Macro %IF-%THEN performs text processing to determine what SAS code to place on the input stack for tokenization, compilation, and execution.

SAS IF-THEN performs data processing to determine whether to execute SAS statements during each execution-time iteration of the DATA step.

30

5.03 Quiz – Correct Answer

Instead of using multiple OR operators, what operator can you use in the DATA step to determine whether a variable value is in a list?

The IN operator can be used in a DATA step for comparisons.

40

5.04 Quiz – Correct Answer

Open program **m105d05c**. How is the macro variable LIST assigned its value?

```
proc sql noprint;
   select distinct country into :list separated by ' '
      from orion.customer;
quit;
```

45

5.05 Multiple Choice Poll – Correct Answer

Which statement correctly creates an index variable
named **i**?

a. %do &i=1 %to 10;
b. %do &i=1   to 10;
c. %do i=1 %to 10;
d. %do i=1   to 10;

64

5.06 Quiz – Correct Answer

Given the symbol table below, what is the value
of &&SITE&COUNT?

```
SPLIT SITE4 IL
SPLIT DATA orion.customer
SPLIT COUNT 7
SPLIT VAR country
SPLIT SITE3 DE
SPLIT SITE2 CA
SPLIT SITE1 AU
SPLIT SITE7 ZA
SPLIT SITE6 US
SPLIT SITE5 TR
```

&&SITE&COUNT ⇨ &SITE7 ⇨ ZA

74

5.07 Quiz – Correct Answer

How many local symbol tables are created when macro A
is called and begins to execute?

```
%macro a(value=);
    %b
%mend a;

%macro b;
    %put The value to write is: &value.;
    %put _user_;
%macro b;

%a(value=Today is Monday)
```

**One. The parameter list in macro A causes a local
symbol table to be created. No local symbol table is
created when macro B is called because macro B
doesn't create local variables.**

103

5.08 Quiz – Correct Answer

Why did you receive a warning message regarding NUM?

**The macro variable NUM was placed into the
NUMOBSL macro's local table and deleted after the
NUMOBSL macro finished execution.**

```
%macro numobsL(lib,dsn);
    options nonotes;
    data _null_;
        call symputx('num', number);
        stop;
        set &lib..&dsn nobs=number;
    run;
    options notes;
%mend numobsL;

%numobsL(orion,order_fact);
%put --->  &num observations;
```

116

Solutions to Chapter Review

Chapter Review – Correct Answers

1. What macro language statements perform conditional processing?

   %IF/%THEN and %ELSE statements

2. Which option causes the SAS log to display the results of arithmetic and logical operations?

   OPTIONS MLOGIC;

3. When is the global symbol table created?

   At SAS initialization

4. When is the global symbol table deleted?

   At SAS termination

130

Chapter Review – Correct Answers

5. Which statement adds several macro variables with null values to the global symbol table?

   %GLOBAL

6. Where can a %LOCAL statement be used?

   Inside a macro definition only

7. When is a local symbol table created?

   When a macro with a parameter list is called or a local macro variable is created during macro execution

8. When is a local symbol table deleted?

   At macro termination

132

Chapter 6 Learning More

6.1   **SAS Resources**...6-3

6.2   **Beyond This Course**...6-6

6.1   SAS Resources

Objectives

- Identify areas of support that SAS offers.

3

Education

Comprehensive training to deliver greater value
to your organization

- More than 200 course offerings
- World-class instructors
- Multiple delivery methods: instructor-led and
  self-paced
- Training centers around the world

http://support.sas.com/training/

4

SAS Publishing

SAS offers a complete selection of publications to help customers use SAS software to its fullest potential:

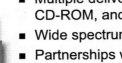

- Multiple delivery methods: e-books, CD-ROM, and hard-copy books
- Wide spectrum of topics
- Partnerships with outside authors, other publishers, and distributors

http://support.sas.com/publishing/

5

SAS Global Certification Program

SAS offers several globally recognized certifications.

- Computer-based certification exams – typically 60-70 questions and 2-3 hours in length
- Preparation materials and practice exams available
- Worldwide directory of SAS Certified Professionals

http://support.sas.com/certify/

6

Support

SAS provides a variety of self-help and assisted-help resources.

- SAS Knowledge Base
- Downloads and hot fixes
- License assistance
- SAS discussion forums
- SAS Technical Support

http://support.sas.com/techsup/

7

User Groups

SAS supports many local, regional, international, and special-interest SAS user groups.

- SAS Global Forum
- Online SAS Community: www.sasCommunity.org

http://support.sas.com/usergroups/

8

6.2 Beyond This Course

Objectives

- Identify the next course that follows this course.

10

Next Steps

To learn advanced macro application development
techniques, enroll in the following course:

SAS® Macro Language 2: Developing Macro Applications

11

Next Steps

In addition, there are prerecorded short technical discussions and demonstrations called e-lectures.

http://support.sas.com/training/

12

Appendix A Supplemental Materials

A.1   Program Flow... **A-3**

A.1 Program Flow

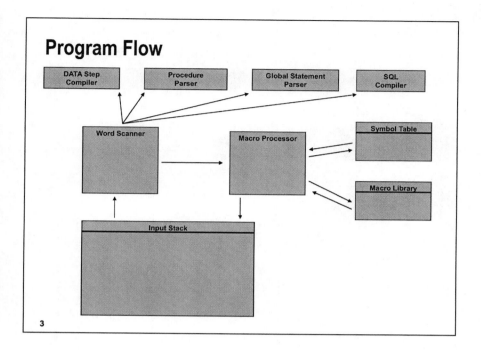

Appendix B Index

%

%DO %UNTIL statement
   syntax, 5-42
%DO %WHILE statement
   syntax, 5-42
%DO statement, 5-10
%ELSE statement
   syntax, 5-5
%END statement, 5-10
%EVAL function, 2-59, 2-67
   syntax, 2-66
%GLOBAL statement
   syntax, 5-49
%IF-%THEN statements
   syntax, 5-5
%INCLUDE statement, 5-11–5-12
   syntax, 5-12
%INDEX function, 2-59
   syntax, 5-25
   validating parameters, 5-26
%LET statement
   execution, 4-7
   trimming blanks, 4-49
%LOCAL statement
   syntax, 5-52
%NRSTR function, 2-59, 2-73
%PUT statement, 1-24
   syntax, 1-24
%SCAN function, 2-59
   syntax, 2-63
%STR function, 2-59, 2-72
   syntax, 2-72
%SUBSTR function, 2-59
   syntax, 2-61
%SYMDEL statement
   syntax, 2-45
%SYSFUNC function, 2-59, 2-68–2-70
   syntax, 2-68
%UPCASE function, 2-59

A

autocall facility, 3-42–3-49
   accessing macros, 3-46–3-47
   calling macros, 3-48

saving macros, 3-48
   system options, 3-43–3-44
   UNIX, 3-45
   Windows, 3-45
   z/OS, 3-45
autocall libraries, 3-42
   defining, 3-43
autocall macros
   accessing, 3-46–3-47
   advantages, 3-49
automatic macro variables, 1-9
   global symbol table, 2-4
   SYSDATE9, 2-69
   SYSTIME, 2-69

C

CALL SYMPUTX statement
   syntax, 4-9, 4-13, 4-16, 4-32
calling macros, 3-7
character string manipulation functions, 2-59
   arguments to, 2-59
compiled macros
   storing, 3-40–3-41
compiler, 1-15
compiling macros, 3-5
conditional iteration, 5-42–5-44
conditional processing, 1-10, 5-4–5-26
   %ELSE statement, 5-5
   %IF-%THEN statements, 5-5
creating macro variables in SQL, 4-49–4-57

D

DATA step interface, 4-4–4-7
data-driven applications, 1-11
defining macros, 3-4–3-5
delimiters
   macro variables, 2-52–2-55

E

executing macros, 3-17–3-18

F

Forward Rescan Rule, 4-35

G

generating data-dependent code, 5-36–5-41
generating SAS code iteratively, 5-35–5-41
global macro variables
  creating, 5-49
global symbol table, 5-48–5-49
  automatic macro variables, 2-4
  characteristics of macro variables, 2-5
  user-defined macro variables, 2-4

I

indirect references to macro variables, 4-27–4-38
input stack, 1-14
INTO clause
  SQL procedure, 4-49–4-57
  syntax, 4-49, 4-52

K

keyword parameters, 3-28–3-31

L

literal tokens, 1-18
local macro variables, 5-50
  creating, 5-51
  using instead of global variables, 5-51
local symbol table, 3-25, 5-50–5-52
  multiple tables, 5-55–5-64

M

macro calls
  syntax, 3-7
  syntax (keyword parameters), 3-28
  syntax (positional parameters), 3-24
macro definitions, 3-4–3-5
  syntax (keyword parameters), 3-28
  syntax (positional parameters), 3-24
macro expressions
  comparing to SAS expressions, 5-5
macro facility
  overview, 1-8
macro functions, 2-58–2-73
macro parameters, 3-23
  keyword, 3-28–3-31
  local symbol table, 3-25
  macro calls, 3-24
  mixed parameter lists, 3-33–3-34
  positional, Error! Not a valid bookmark in entry on page 3-23, 3-26–3-27

validating, 5-21–5-24
validating with the %INDEX function, 5-26
macro processor, 1-21–1-23, 1-26
  macro variable references, 2-10
macro statements, 1-23
  executing iteratively, 5-30–5-33
macro syntax errors, 5-10
macro triggers, 1-21
macro variable references
  substitution within macro statements, Error! Not a valid bookmark in entry on page 2-15
  substitution within SAS code, Error! Not a valid bookmark in entry on page 2-24
  substitution within SAS literals, 2-15
  unresolved, 2-25–2-27
macro variables
  automatic, 1-9, 2-4
  combining with text, 2-49–2-50
  creating a series of, 4-31–4-33
  creating in SQL, 4-49–4-57
  creating in the DATA step, 4-4–4-20
  delimiters, 2-52–2-55
  delimiting references, 2-48–2-55
  global, 5-49
  indirect references to, 4-27–4-38
  introduction, 2-3–2-5
  local, 5-50
  references, 2-10–2-26
  referencing, 2-48
  retrieving in the DATA step, 4-43–4-46
  rules for creating, 5-53
  rules for resolving, 5-53
  rules for updating, 5-53
  user-defined, 1-9, 2-4, 2-31–2-44
macro-level programming, 5-4
macros
  calling, 3-7
  compiling, 3-5
  defining, 3-4–3-5
  efficiency, 1-11
  executing, 3-17–3-18
  program flow, 3-10–3-17, A-3
  storage, 3-6
  storing compiled, 3-40–3-41
MAUTOSOURCE system option, 3-43
MCOMPILENOTE= option
  syntax, 3-5
mixed parameter lists, 3-33–3-34
MLOGIC system option, 5-8

syntax, 5-6
MPRINT option, 3-18
MSTORED system option, 3-40

N

name tokens, 1-17
NOMLOGIC system option
   syntax, 5-6
number tokens, 1-18

P

positional parameters, Error! Not a valid
   bookmark in entry on page 3-23, 3-26–3-
   27
processing complete statements, 5-13–5-15
processing partial statements, 5-17
program flow, 1-14–1-15, 3-10–3-17, A-3
PUT function, 4-18
PUTN function, 4-20

R

repetitive processing, 1-10
retrieving macro variables in the DATA
   step, 4-43–4-46

S

SAS code
   generating iteratively, 5-35–5-41
SAS DATA step
   creating macro variables, 4-4–4-20
SASAUTOS= system option, 3-43–3-44
   syntax, 3-44
SASMSTORE= system option, 3-40
simple loops, 5-30–5-33
SOURCE2 option
   %INCLUDE statement, 5-12
special tokens, 1-17
special WHERE operators, 5-5
SQL procedure
   INTO clause, 4-49–4-54, 4-49–4-57
STORE option, 3-41
stored compiled macros, 3-40–3-41
   advantages, 3-49

permanent, 3-41
SYMBOLGEN system option, 5-8
symbolic variables, 2-3
SYMGET function, 4-43–4-46
   syntax, 4-44
SYMPUT routine, 4-13
SYMPUTX routine, 4-9–4-18
   controlling with DATA step execution-
      time logic, 4-10
   copying the value of a DATA step
      variable, 4-13
   creating a series of macro variables, 4-31–
      4-33
   formatting data values, 4-16–4-18
SYSDATE9 automatic macro variables, 2-69
system values
   substituting, 1-9
SYSTIME automatic macro variables, 2-69

T

table lookup application, 4-27–4-30
tokenization, 1-16–1-18
tokens
   classes of, 1-16–1-18
trimming blanks
   %LET statement, 4-49

U

unresolved references, 2-25–2-27
user-defined macro variables, 1-9, 2-4
   %LET statement, 2-32–2-40
   deleting, 2-45
   global symbol table, 2-4
user-defined values
   substituting, 1-9

V

validating parameters, 5-21–5-24, 5-26

W

word scanner, 1-15
   classes of tokens recognized, 1-16